ALL
ABOUT
SIN

ALL ABOUT SIN

Compiled by Peter Potter

Published by
William Mulvey Inc.
72 Park Street
New Canaan, Conn. 06840

Cover design: Ted Palmer

Library of Congress Cataloging-in-Publication Data

All About Sin
"A Bull's-eye Book"

Includes index.
1. Sin—Quotations, maxims, etc.
I. Potter, Peter (date).

BT715.A45   1988   170   86−43158

ISBN 0−934791−09−0

All Scriptural quotations are from the
King James Version of the Bible.
ABS 1967   KJ053-C   Series−D−2

Printed in the United States of America
First Edition

Dedicated to the Clergy.
Men and Women who give their lives
so we can better know Jesus Christ.

Introduction

Sin? What is it?

The dictionary says sin is "any voluntary transgression of a religious law or moral principle."

To most of us, sin is much simpler—it's doing certain things that are wrong. And there are degrees of sin. There are venial sins. And there are mortal sins.

This fascinating subject of sin has intrigued thinking men and women for centuries. What did they think of sin? What did they say about sin?

Here are their observations. I think you'll find their thoughts stimulating.

Peter Potter

Adultery
Appearances

Adultery

They are foes of mutual fidelity who teach that the ideas prevailing at the present time concerning false and harmful relations with a third party can be tolerated, and that a greater freedom of feeling and action should be permitted to man or wife.

Pope Pius XI

When dealing with adultery becomes a matter of private choice instead of public rules, middle-class morality, that bastion of social stability, has ceased to function.

Elizabeth Janeway

Society, when it rules "thumbs down" on extramarital relations, is guarding itself against destruction.

Mario A. Castallo

To leave a wife who is sterile in order to take another by whom children may be had. Anyone doing this is guilty of adultery.

Saint Augustine of Hippo

Whosoever shall put away his wife, saving for the cause of fornication, causeth her to commit adultery: and whosoever shall marry her that is divorced committeth adultery.

The Bible

Adultery is an evil only inasmuch as it is a theft; but we do not steal that which is given to us.

Voltaire

The adulterer is a more grievous offender than the thief.

Saint John Chrysostom

When cheated, wife or husband feels the same.

Euripides

Those who are faithful know only the trivial side of love; it is the faithless who know love's tragedies.

Oscar Wilde

If a married woman shall be caught lying with another man, both shall be bound and thrown into the river.

Code of Hammurabi

There is nothing which Allah abhors more than adultery. The eye and the tongue can commit adultery.

The Koran

I've looked on a lot of women with lust. I've committed adultery in my heart many times. This is something God recognizes I will do—and I have done it—and God forgives me for it. But that doesn't mean that I condemn someone who not only looks on a woman with lust but who leaves his wife and shacks up with someone out of wedlock.

Jimmy Carter

It shall be considered adultery to offer presents to a married woman, to romp with her, to touch her dress or ornaments, or to sit with her on a bed.

Code of Manu

If thou marry, thou hast not sinned; and if a virgin marry, she hath not sinned. Nevertheless such shall have trouble in the flesh: but I spare you.

The Bible

There is no worse adultery than that of the woman who, while making love with her husband, thinks of another man.

Midrash

Adultery is usually an act done under cover of darkness and secrecy, and in which the parties are seldom surprised.

Maryland Court of Appeals

5

. . .one of the most frequent causes of adultery: the longing a transparent man feels to become opaque. He suddenly finds himself wrapped in mystery, as if he had bought a new suit. This mystery is most becoming; it conceals the fact that the left shoulder is lower than the right, it nips in the waist, it makes the leg more slender. Oh, it's a marvelous tailor! The unexpected new suit makes you look fifteen years younger.

Jean Dutourd

It is the fear of middle-age in the young, of old-age in the middle-aged, which is the prime cause of infidelity, that infallible rejuvenator.

Cyril Connoly

The way of the adulterer is hedged with thorns; full of fears and jealousies, burning desires and impatient waitings, tediousness of delay and suffrance of affronts, and amazements of discovery.

Jeremy Taylor

Appearances

There are some faults which bear witness to a good character more clearly than some virtues.

Cardinal de Retz (Jean-François Paul de Gondi)

One should seek for the salutary in the unpleasant; if it is
there, it is after all nectar. One should seek for the deceitful in
the pleasant; if it is there, it is after all poison.

Panchatantra

No one is so wicked that he wants to seem wicked.

Quintilian

Avoid the appearance of evil; it is harder to live down than
evil.

Anonymous

Always do right. This will gratify some people and astonish
the rest.

Mark Twain (Samuel Clemens)

A private sin is not so prejudicial in this world as a public
indecency.

Cervantes

The devil's most devilish when respectable.

Elizabeth Barrett Browning

Some people with great virtues are disagreeable, while others
with great vices are delightful.

La Rochefoucauld

7

He is a saint trying unsuccessfully to be a sinner, and I am a sinner trying equally unsuccessfully to be a saint.

Malcolm Muggeridge

A saloon won't harm a good man, a synagogue won't help a bad one.

Hebrew proverb

B

Bad Examples
Bad Habits
Bad Intentions
Blame
Boredom

Bad Examples

We sometimes learn more from the sight of evil than from an example of good; and it is well to accustom ourselves to profit by the evil which is so common, while that which is good is so rare.

Blaise Pascal

When you see a good man, think of emulating him; when you see a bad man, examine your own heart.

Confucius

We are quick to copy what is base and depraved.

Juvenal

The wrong that men do can all be traced to those who mis-taught them.

Sophocles

Sin would be only an evil for him who commits it, were it not a crime towards the weak brethren, whom it corrupts.

Henri Amiel

It is good to see in another's evil the things that we should flee from.

Publilius Syrus

The man who backbites an absent friend, nay, who does not stand up for him when another blames him, the man who angles for bursts of laughter and for the repute of a wit, who can invent what he never saw, who cannot keep a secret—that man is black at heart: mark and avoid him, if you are a Roman.

Cicero

It is better to be alone than in bad company.

George Washington

I see the better course and approve it; I follow the worse.

Ovid

He that walketh with wise men shall be wise: but a companion of fools shall be destroyed.

The Bible

As one virtue bringeth in another, so one vice nourisheth another; pride engendereth envy, and idleness is an entrance into lust.

John Northbrooke

The act of evil breeds others to follow, young sins in its own likeness.

Aeschylus

Bad Habits

Every sin, the oftener it is committed, the more it acquireth in the quality of evil; as it succeeds in time, so it proceeds in degrees of badness; for as they proceed they ever multiply, and, like figures in arithmetic, the last stands for more than all that went before it.

Thomas Browne

No sin is too big for God to pardon, and none too small for habit to magnify.

Bahya ben Joseph ibn Pakuda

Every evil in the bud is easily crushed; as it grows older, it becomes stronger.

Cicero

If a man commits a sin, let him not do it again; let him not delight in it, for the accumulation of evil is painful.

Dhammapada

If once a man indulges himself in murder, very soon he comes to think little of robbing; and from robbing he comes next to drinking and Sabbath-breaking, and from that to incivility and procrastination.

Thomas De Quincey

It is a great deal easier to commit a second sin than it was to commit the first, and a great deal harder to repent of a second than it was to repent of the first.

Benjamin Whichcote

He who has committed a sin twice considers it no longer a sin.

The Talmud

There are some vices which only keep hold on us through other ones, and if we take the trunk away they come off like the branches.

Blaise Pascal

The curse of an evil deed is that it must always continue to engender evil.

Ferdinand C. S. Schiller

Sin is energy in the wrong channel.

Saint Augustine of Hippo

The big moment is not when a man sins but when a man surrenders to the direction of his sin.

Hubert Van Zeller

Three things sap a man's strength: worry, travel, and sin.

The Talmud

I don't drink, don't carouse and don't fool around with
women. These things are all bad for you.

Eubie Blake

Samson with his strong body had a weak head, or he would
not have laid it in a harlot's lap.

Benjamin Franklin

Bad Intentions

A truth that's told with bad intent
Beats all the lies you can invent.

William Blake

A sinner is like a man who sees open manacles—and puts his
hands in them.

The Talmud

I loathe women who boast of their chastity, while secretly
daring every sin.

Euripides

A whore is like a crocodile that fastens upon her prey with her
tail.

Samuel Butler

Thoughts invite us, more than words and deeds, to continue in sin, for thoughts can be concealed, while words and deeds cannot.

Søren Kierkegaard

He who is bent on doing evil can never lack occasion.

Publilius Syrus

How many men sin over the sins of their youth again in their old age, by a sinful delight in remembering those sins, and a sinful desire that their bodies were not past them?

John Donne

The mere wish to sin entails the penalty. For he who meditates a crime within his breast has all the guilt of the deed.

Juvenal

Every judge who has accepted bribes weighs truth badly.

Horace

We are no more responsible for the evil thoughts that pass through our minds than a scarecrow for the birds which fly over the seedplot he has to guard. The sole responsibility in each case is to prevent them from settling.

Churton Collins

Don't kindle the coals of a sinner: you may be scorched by the flames of his fire.

Ben Sirach

Our transgression is in our thoughts. It is pure chance if these thoughts become deeds, if they materialize.

Georg Büchner

The sins of the mind are the last habitation of the devil.

Jarol Johnson

Who is the most diligent bishop and prelate in England?. . .I will tell you. It is the devil. . . . He is never out of his diocese. . . . The devil is diligent at his plough.

Hugh Latimer

Sin is the purposeful disobedience of a creature to the known will of God.

F. L. Cross

Really to sin you have to be serious about it.

Henrik Ibsen

Blame

Men are no doubt involuntary sinners in the sense that they do not actually desire to sin; but this does not alter the fact that wrong-doers, of their own choice, are, themselves, the agents; it is because they themselves act that the sin is in their own; if they were not agents they could not sin.

Plotinus

Why blame the world? The world is free
Of sin; the blame is yours and mine.

Abu'l-Ala-al-Ma'arri

Every man carries the bundle of his sins
Upon his own back.

John Fletcher

When thou art preparing to commit a sin, think not that thou wilt conceal it; there is a God that forbids crimes to be hidden.

Tibullus

The corruption of the age is made up by the particular contribution of every individual man; some contribute treachery, others injustice, irreligion, tyranny, avarice, cruelty, according to their power.

Montaigne

Three elements. . .first, that the deed was one that ought not to have been done. . .because it was opposed to what is intrinsically right. . . .Secondly, the idea of sin implies that the sinner himself is the doer of the deed. . .. Thirdly, it is the characteristic of sin that the fuller knowledge that the harmful deed is sinful comes after the act.

Felix Adler

Excellence of the person never diminishes sin; but on the contrary increases it. Therefore a sin is not less grievous in a believer than an unbeliever, but much more so. For the sins of an unbeliever are more deserving of forgiveness on account of their ignorance.

Saint Thomas Aquinas

One sinner destroyeth much good.

The Bible

To sin is to poison the public reservoir.

Leslie D. Weatherhead

Much of the most important evils that mankind have to consider are those which they inflict upon each other through stupidity or malevolence or both.

Bertrand Russell

Boredom

There ain't any news in being good. You might write the doings of all the convents of the world on the back of a postage stamp, and have room to spare.

Finley P. Dunne

Science may have found a cure for most evils: but it has found no remedy for the worst of them all—the apathy of human beings.

Helen Keller

Boredom is a vital problem for the moralist, since at least half the sins of mankind are caused by the fear of it.

Bertrand Russell

Who's free to sin, sins less: the very power robs evildoing of its choicest flavor.

Ovid

Our sins, like to our shadows,
When our day is in its glory, scarce appear:
Toward our evening how great and monstrous
They are!

John Suckling

Sin is disappointing. Whoever got out of sin half as much pleasure as he expected?

Ignatius Smith

The pleasure of sin is of short duration. . . . It operates on a law of diminishing returns. The more often it is repeated, the more familiar with its face, the less pleasure sin gives.

Ignatius Smith

To know the good is to react against the bad. Indifference is the mark of deprivation.

Marya Mannes

My sins are not scarlet, they are grey—all grey.

William Temple

C

Casting The First Stone
Chastity
Choice
Compromises
Confession
Conscience
Conscience Stricken
Consequences
Corruption

Casting The First Stone

When you look over your own vices, winking at them, as it were, with sore eyes; why are you with regard to those of your friends as sharp-sighted as an eagle, or the Epidaurian serpent?

Horace

If we desire to judge all things justly, we must first persuade ourselves that none of us is without sin.

Seneca

He that is without sin among you, let him first cast a stone at her.

The Bible

The virtue of some people consists wholly in condemning the vices of others.

Herbert Samuel

Don't condemn the sinner! We are, or we were, or we could be as this man is.

Thomas Hearne

You will not become a saint through other people's sins.

Anton Chekhov

We have committed some sins; others we have considered committing. Some we have desired; others we have encouraged. Some transgressions we are innocent of only because they did not succeed. With this in mind, we should be more forbearing toward transgressors and pay more attention to those who reprove us.

Seneca

A moralist criticizes other people's sins, a saint criticizes his own.

Anonymous

There is no witness so terrible, no accuser so potent, as the conscience that dwells in every man's breast.

Polybius

The sins that we should hate most are not those of our neighbor but our own. These are the only sins over which God has given us immediate power.

Raphael Simon

There are a thousand hacking at the branches of evil to one who is striking at the root.

Henry David Thoreau

Let us not therefore judge one another any more: but judge this rather, that no man put a stumbling block or an occasion to fall in his brother's way.

The Bible

Resolved, never to reprove another except I experience at the same time a peculiar contrition of heart.

Henry Martyn

Chastity

Is continency preferable to marriage? A life of perfect chastity, embraced for God's sake, is a better and more blessed state.

John McCaffrey

Chastity is the cement of civilization and progress.

Mary Baker Eddy

The chastity of widows and virgins is above the chastity of marriage.

Saint Augustine of Hippo

All women are chaste where there are no men.

Sanskrit proverb

You may say. . .we need not expect young men to live up to ideal of continence. If so, I cannot agree. It is a duty we cannot shirk to point to the true ideal, to chastity, to a single standard of morals for men and women.

Josephus Daniels

We Christians regard a stain upon our chastity as more dreadful than any punishment, or even than death itself.

Tertullian

Set chastity above life itself.

Aeschylus

If you can't be chaste, be careful.

Latin proverb

Chastity, the lily of virtues, makes men almost equal to angels. Nothing is beautiful but what is pure, and the purity of men is chastity.

Saint Francis of Sales

Temperance is the nurse of chastity.

William Wycherley

There never was a drunken woman, or a woman who loved strong drink, who was chaste, if the opportunity of being the contrary presented itself to her.

William Cobbett

Beauty and chastity are always quarreling.

Spanish proverb

The most virtuous woman always has something within her that is not quite chaste.

Honoré de Balzac

A reputation for chastity is necessary to a woman. Chastity itself is also sometimes useful.

Anonymous

Is not chastity a virtue? Most undoubtedly, and a virtue of high deserving. And why? Not because it diminishes, but because it heightens enjoyment.

Jeremy Bentham

Choice

God is not dead, but neither is Satan.

Clate A. Risley

Why didn't God create the universe without sin? There is only one answer: He could have done so, and man would have been but a pawn upon a chessboard. Pawns are not responsible for moves of the great Player. We must be free to be persons, and being free, we are charged with making decisions.

G. Bromley Oxnam

God predestines every man to be saved. The devil predestines every man to be damned. Man has the casting vote.

Anonymous

We cannot freely and wisely choose the right way for ourselves unless we know both good and evil.

Helen Keller

If a man is tempted, he has a chance to choose and thereby become a worthier man. Temptation is thus a fork in the road, a way up or a way down; and if God is man's Unseen Ally, temptation can be a blessing.

George A. Buttrick

All I maintain is that on this earth there are pestilences and there are victims, and it's up to us, as far as possible, not to join forces with the pestilences.

Albert Camus

Free will is granted to every man. If he wishes to direct himself toward the good way and become righteous, the will to do so is in his hand; and if he wishes to direct himself toward the bad way and become wicked, the will to do so is likewise in his hand.

Maimonides

I would rather dwell with a lion or serpent than with an evil woman.

Ben Sirach

When God sends us evil, he sends with it the weapon to
conquer it.

Paul V. Carroll

If a man has a right to find God in his own way, he has a right
to go to the Devil in his own way also.

Hugh M. Hefner

Dishonesty, cowardice, and duplicity are never impulsive.

George A. Knight

The heroic hours of life do not announce their presence by
drum and trumpet, challenging us to be true to ourselves by
appeals to the martial spirit that keeps the blood at heat.
Some little, unassuming, unobtrusive choice presents itself
before us slyly and craftily, glib and insinuating, in the modest garb of innocence. To yield to its blandishments is so easy.
The wrong, it seems, is venial. . . .Then it is that you will be
summoned to show the courage of adventurous youth.

Benjamin Cardozo

It is better to be called a fool all of one's days than to sin for
one hour.

Hebrew proverb

White shall not neutralize the black nor good;
Compensate bad in man, absolve him so;
Life's business being just the terrible choice.

Robert Browning

Men and nations sink or soar, survive or perish, as they choose to be dominated by sin or righteousness.

A. P. Gouthey

The power of choosing good and evil is within the reach of all.

Origen

Compromises

Nurse one vice in your bosom. Give it the attention it deserves and let your virtues spring up modestly around it. Then you'll have the miser who's no liar; and the drunkard who's the benefactor of a whole city.

Thornton Wilder

The sinner wills a good, an advantage, and to obtain it he freely consents to turn away from his final end: this is the evil of sin.

Saint Thomas Aquinas

Fools! who from hence into the notion fall
That Vice or Virtue there is none at all.
If white and black blend, soften, and unite
A thousand ways, is there no black or white?

Alexander Pope

A good end cannot sanctify evil means; nor must we ever do evil, that good may come of it.

William Penn

▬▬▬

If someone tells you he is going to make "a realistic decision", you immediately understand that he has resolved to do something bad.

Mary McCarthy

▬▬▬

He who passively accepts evil is as much involved in it as he who helps to perpetrate it. He who accepts evil without protesting against it is really cooperating with it.

Martin Luther King, Jr.

▬▬▬

There are some jobs in which it is impossible for a man to be virtuous.

Aristotle

▬▬▬

You cannot drive straight on a twisting lane.

Russian proverb

Confession

He that covereth his sins shall not prosper: but whoso confesseth and forsaketh them shall have mercy.

The Bible

Forgive me my sins, O Lord; forgive me the sins of my youth and the sins of mine age, the sins of my soul and the sins of my body, my secret and my whispering sins, the sins I have done to please myself and the sins I have done to please others. Forgive those sins which I know, and the sins which I know not; forgive them, O Lord, forgive them all of Thy great goodness.

Anonymous

History proves that deeply religious people of all ages have felt the need to reveal their guilt not only before God, but to make timely confessions of their wrongdoing before men. Contemporary psychological research is verifying the therapeutic value of open admission of guilt to others.

Bernard Haring

The confession of evil works is the first beginning of good works.

Saint Augustine of Hippo

A sin confessed is half forgiven.

John Ray

A fault confessed is a new virtue added to a man.

James S. Knowles

For him who confesses, shams are over and realities have begun.

William James

34

O God, thou knowest my foolishness;
and my sins are not hid from thee.

The Bible

Owning her weakness,
Her evil behaviour,
And leaving with meekness,
Her sins to her Saviour!

Thomas Hood

Should we all confess our sins to one another we would all
laugh at one another for our lack of originality.

Kahlil Gibran

Against thee, thee only, have I sinned,
and done this evil in thy sight.

The Bible

We have left undone those things
    which we ought to have done;
And we have done those things which
    we ought not to have done.

Book of Common Prayer

Conscience

The moral sense, or conscience, is as much a part of man as his leg and arm.

Thomas Jefferson

Everyone has an inner conscience . . . . The cynic who ridicules conscience forgets that his own cynicism has its reason not unrelated to his conscience. The rabid behavior of the cynic is the expression of defensive warfare against his "internal enemy." He strikes others, but he is aiming at himself.

Edmund Bergler

The greatest event in natural history was the birth of conscience in the human mind. That was the moment when man put aside his strongest natural instinct, which was self-interest.

Lecomte Du Noüy

Temptation is the voice of the suppressed evil; conscience is the voice of the repressed good.

J. A. Hadfield

More potent than all the brass-buttoned policemen in the land is the restraining power of conscience.

John A. O'Brien

Conscience is the inner voice that warns us somebody may be looking.

H. L. Mencken

The beautiful idea that every man has with him a Guardian Angel is true indeed: for Conscience is ever on the watch, ever ready to warn us of danger.

John Lubbock

Every conscience, whether it be true or faulty, and whether it is concerned with bad acts or indifferent acts, is binding, and therefore anyone who acts against his conscience commits sin.

Saint Thomas Aquinas

Conscience warns us before it reproaches us.

Diane de Poitiers

Not to hear conscience is the way to silence it.

Thomas Fuller

A quiet conscience sleeps in thunder.

Thomas Fuller

Reason often makes mistakes, but conscience never does.

Josh Billings (Henry Wheeler Shaw)

Conscience that can see without light sits in the areopagy and dark tribunal of our hearts, surveying our thoughts and condemning their obliquities.

Thomas Browne

Throughout eternity an infinite stillness reigns wherein the conscience may talk with the individual. . . . It must be heard.

Søren Kierkegaard

Conscience cannot be cajoled. It cannot be bribed. It cannot be coerced. It cannot be silenced. It can be disobeyed. For man is a free agent. But it cannot be disobeyed with impunity.

John A. O'Brien

Conscience is a mother-in-law whose visit never ends.

H. L. Mencken

Conscience Stricken

Men conceive they can manage their sins with secrecy; but they carry about them a letter, or book rather, written by God's finger, their conscience bearing witness to all their actions.

Thomas Fuller

Sin can be well-guarded, but free from anxiety it cannot be.

Seneca

My conscience is more trouble and bother to me than anything else I started with.

> Mark Twain (Samuel Clemens)

The evil-doer suffers in this world, and he suffers in the next;
he suffers in both. He suffers when he thinks of the evil he has
done; he suffers more when going on the evil path.

> Dhammapada

Conscience can become hardened like water becoming
ice. . . . It films over gradually, and at last becomes hard:
and then it can bear a weight of iniquity.

> Sebastian Miklas

The decrees of conscience are not judgments but feelings.

> Jean-Jacques Rousseau

Some have sinned with safety, but none with peace of soul.

> Seneca

He that loses his conscience has nothing left that is worth
keeping.

> Nicolas Caussin

Conscience is thoroughly well-bred, and soon leaves off talking to those who do not wish to hear it.

> Samuel Butler

A clear conscience welcomes a crowd, but a bad conscience is disturbed and troubled even in solitude.

Seneca

Consequences

There are no national virtues. We are alone, each one of us. If we are good, the virtues of others will not make us better. We cannot borrow morals.

Aubrey Menen

We gather the consequences of our own deeds. Body of mine, repay what you have done!

Garuda Purana (Pali)

Good and evil do not befall men without reason. Heaven sends them happiness or misery according to their conduct.

Confucius

It matters not how a man dies, but how he lives.

Samuel Johnson

The promises of sin are fair but the payoff is cruel.

Albert Nielsen

It is the fear of punishment either of the king, or of hell, or of society that keeps people away from sin.

Mahabharata

Sin in his (Buddha's) opinion is essentially irrational conduct; conduct that tends to destroy more values than it creates, either for the actor or other sentient beings whom it affects.

J. B. Pratt

The sins committed by many pass unpunished.

Lucan

The success of the wicked is a temptation to many others.

Phaedrus

It is folly to punish your neighbor by fire when you live next door.

Publilius Syrus

It is beyond man's power to explain the prosperity of the wicked, or the troubles of the good.

Saying of the Fathers

The happiness of the wicked glides away like a stream.

Jean Racine

Though hand join in hand, the wicked shall not be unpunished.
The Bible

Vice stings us even in our pleasures, but virtue consoles us even in our pains.

Charles C. Colton

Sin makes its own hell, and goodness its own heaven.
Mary Baker Eddy

Better is a little with righteousness, than great revenues without right.

The Bible

Hell can have no terror for the poor sinner who has got himself married to a saint.

Anonymous

Curses are like processions; they return to the place from which they came.

Giovanni Ruffini

The wicked borroweth, and payeth not again:
but the righteous showeth mercy, and giveth.

The Bible

The evil that men do lives after them;
The good is oft interred with their bones.

Shakespeare

Corruption

What it comes down to is this: the grocer, the butcher, the baker, the merchant, the landlord, the druggist, the liquor dealer, the policeman, the doctor, the city father and the politician—these are the people who make money out of prostitution, these are the real reapers of the wages of sin.

Polly Adler

There is something in corruption which, like a jaundiced eye, transfers the color of itself to the object it looks upon and sees everything stained and impure.

Thomas Paine

A hurtful act is the transference to others of the degradation which we bear in ourselves.

Simone Weil

Prostitution is . . . the very core of the female's social condition. . . . It is not sex the prostitute is really made to see: it is degradation.

Kate Millett

43

If you try to cleanse others, you will waste away in the process, like soap.

Madagascan proverb

Everything is filthy to him who has filthy hands.

Bertolt Brecht

We tolerate without rebuke the vices with which we have grown familiar.

Publilius Syrus

Tremble before committing a minor sin, for it may lead you to a major one.

The Talmud

Evil enters like a needle and spreads like an oak tree.

Ethiopian proverb

Power corrupts the few, while weakness corrupts the many.

Eric Hoffer

A man without ethics is a wild beast loosed upon this world.

Manly P. Hall

We have sinned and grown old and our Father is younger than we.

G. K. Chesterton

Let no man think of evil, saying in his heart, it will not come nigh unto me. Even by the falling of water-drops a water-pot is filled; the fool becomes full of evil even if he gather it little by little.

Dhammapada

Sin penetrates the soul as a needle does the body; for this will work its way for years, slowly and surely, till it pierces an intestine, or even the heart itself.

Walter Elliott

Sin is poison poured into the stream of time.

George A. Buttrick

Corruption is like a ball of snow; whence once set a-rolling it must increase.

Charles C. Colton

A slight failing in one virtue is enough to put all the others to sleep.

Saint Teresa of Avila

Sin, the sad fearful winter of the soul, kills the holy works which it finds there.

Saint Francis of Sales

Knowledge alone does not stop men from evil. The poor and the ignorant are not the greatest sinners. Man's mind may unfold, his intellect grow more keen, his understanding more profound, yet side by side with this may be a moral degeneration such as existed in pagan Greece and Rome.

William A. Scully

No sin is small. No grain of sand is small in the mechanism of a watch.

Jeremy Taylor

D

Damnation
Denial
Despair
Devil's Work
Discipline
Doubt
Duty

Damnation

The Catholic Church holds that it were better for sun and moon to drop from heaven, for the earth to fail, and for all the many millions who are upon it to die of starvation in extremest agony, as far as temporal affliction goes, than that one soul, I will not say, should be lost, but should commit one single venial sin, should tell one wilful untruth . . . or steal one poor farthing without excuse.

John Henry

To make another man sin is worse than to kill him; for it is to doom him not only in this world but in the next.

Midrash

Sin has done injury, I: to God, II: to oneself, III: to other men, IV: to the Mystical Body, i.e., to the human race, of which the sinner is an integral member.

Alban Goodier

One leak will sink a ship; and one sin will destroy a sinner.

John Bunyan

Hell has three gates; lust, anger, and greed.

Bhagavadgita

Whoever yields to temptation debases himself with a debasement from which he can never rise. A man can be wronged and live; but the unrestricted, unchecked impulse to do wrong is the first and second death.

Horace Mann

Four things does a reckless man gain who covets his neighbor's wife—a bad reputation, an uncomfortable bed, thirdly punishment, and lastly hell.

Dhammapada

Sin pulled angels out of Heaven, pulls men down to Hell, and overthroweth kingdoms.

John Bunyan

The Evil Will lures man in this world, then testifies against him in the world to come.

The Talmud

It is the iron's own rust that destroys it. It is the sinner's own acts that bring him to hell.

Dhammapada

Sin is rebellion against God; it is a traitor's act who aims at the overthrow and death of His sovereign. . . . Sin is the mortal enemy of the All-holy, so that He and it cannot be together.

John H. Newman

The fire of Hell is insupportable—who does not know it?—and its torments are awful. But if you were to heap a thousand hell-fires one on top of the other, it would be as nothing compared to the punishment of being excluded from the beautiful glory of Heaven, hated by Christ and compelled to hear him say, "I know you not."

Saint John Chrysostom

. . . he that hides a dark soul and foul thoughts
Benighted walks under the mid-day sun;
Himself his own dungeon.

Milton

Of these four we all have more than we know: sins, debts, foes, and years.

Persian proverb

A wicked man is his own Hell.

Thomas Fuller

The safest road to Hell is the gradual one—the gentle slope, soft underfoot, without sudden turnings, without milestones, without signposts.

C. S. Lewis

There is a dreadful Hell,
   And everlasting pains;
There sinners must with devils dwell
   In darkness, fire, and chains.

Isaac Watts

That's the greatest torture souls feel in hell:
In hell, that they must live and cannot die.

John Webster

Evil people know each other.

Arab proverb

All spirits are enslaved which serve things evil.

Percy Bysshe Shelley

Verily, verily, I say unto you, Whosoever committeth sin is
the servant of sin.

The Bible

We are in an age of Darkness. The state of outer darkness is
the state of sin—that is, alienation or estrangement from the
inner light.

R. D. Laing

Man is by nature rational. When, therefore, he acts according to reason, he acts of himself and according to his free will; and this is liberty. . . . When he sins, he acts in opposition to reason, is moved by another, and is the victim of foreign misapprehensions. Therefore, whosoever committeth sin is the slave of sin.

Saint Thomas Aquinas

Do what you feel in your heart to be right—for you'll be criticized anyway. You'll be damned if you do, and damned if you don't.

Eleanor Roosevelt

Denial

There are only two kinds of men: the righteous who believe themselves sinners; the rest, sinners, who believe themselves righteous.

Blaise Pascal

You can close your eyes to realities but not to memories.

Stanislaus J. Lec

Only a fool could deny the fact of sin, though we may choose to call it by another name.

Gerald Vann

When you feel that something is wrong and you have a bad
conscience about it, this is not the sin against the Holy Spirit,
but when you sin and have a good conscience about it, this is
the sin against the Holy Spirit.

Martin Luther

Virtues and vices are of a strange nature; for the more we
have, the fewer we think we have.

Anonymous

Such is the way of an adulterous woman; she eateth, and
wipeth her mouth, and saith, I have done no wickedness.

The Bible

Other men' sins are before our eyes; our own are behind our
back.

Seneca

I feel devastated when I think of going before God with
empty hands. It is sin that has turned away from me, not I
from sin.

Liane de Pougy

Man can hardly even recognize the devils of his own creation.

Albert Schweitzer

If I am not finding Jesus a real Savior, who brings me fully out of the darkness and defeat into light and liberty, it is because at one point or another I am not willing to be broken, and see myself as a sinner.

Roy Hession

The final proof of the sinner is that he does not know his own sin.

Martin Luther

The worst of my actions and feelings do not seem to me so offensive as the cowardice of not daring to admit them.

Montaigne

Your sin will find you out.

The Bible

He does not cleanse himself of his sins who denies them.

Latin proverb

Woe unto them that call evil good, and good evil; that put darkness for light, and light for darkness; that put bitter for sweet, and sweet for bitter!

The Bible

Most men, finding themselves the authors of their own disgrace, rail the louder against God or destiny.

Robert Louis Stevenson

———

For that which I do, I allow not: for what I would, that do I not; but what I hate, that do I.

The Bible

Despair

God delights in our temptations, and yet hates them. He delights in them when they drive us to prayer; He hates them when they drive us to despair.

Martin Luther

———

Talk about sin will not be intelligible to one who has no sense of lack, no sense of life's being at cross-purposes, no sense of self-defeat.

James A. Martin

———

For if there is a sin against life, it consists perhaps not so much in despairing of life as in hoping for another life and in eluding the implacable grandeur of this life.

Albert Camus

If there be a pain which devils might pity man for enduring, it is the death-bed reflection that we have possessed the power of doing good, but we have abused and perverted it to the purposes of ill.

Charles C. Colton

He who despairs of pardon for his sin, damns himself by despair rather than by the crime he has committed.

Saint Isidore of Seville

My son, the world is dark with griefs and graves,
So dark that men cry out against the Heavens.
Who knows but that the darkness is in man?

Alfred Lord Tennyson

Devil's Work

Sarcasm I now see to be, in general the language of the Devil; for which reason I have, long since, as good as renounced it.

Thomas Carlyle

God created the world, but it is the Devil who keeps it going.

Tristan Bernard

Temptation is Satan's opening wedge into a man's being. He does not want to stop there. If a man will obey demonic promptings to do evil, Satan will do worse with him by far than merely to tempt him.

McCandlish Phillips

It is easy—terribly easy—to shake a man's faith in himself. To take advantage of that to break a man's spirit is devil's work.

George Bernard Shaw

Weeds always flourish.

Erasmus

The Devil's boots don't crack.

Scottish proverb

Bad company is the devil's net.

Anonymous

The Devil tempts men to be wicked that he may punish them for being so.

Samuel Butler

Sin is disease, deformity, weakness.

Plato

It often needs as much effort to yield as to resist, to do harm as to do good; as many struggles with oneself, no less arduous, and grimmer.

Paul Valéry

The wicked often work harder to go to hell than the righteous do to enter heaven.

Josh Billings (Henry Wheeler Shaw)

What a silly fellow must he be who would do the devil's work for nothing.

Henry Fielding

Discipline

The first idea that the child must acquire, in order to be actively disciplined is that of the difference between good and evil and the task of the educator lies in seeing that the child does not confound good with immobility, and evil with activity.

Maria Montessori

Educate your children to self-control, to the habit of holding passion and prejudice and evil tendencies subject to an upright and reasoning will, and you have done much to abolish misery from their future lives and crimes from society.

Daniel Webster

We should strengthen ourselves against these failings: neglect of godliness; study without understanding; failure to act
up to what we believe to be right; inability to change bad
habits.

Confucius

"Sins" are indispensable to every society organized on an
ecclesiastical basis; they are the only reliable weapons of
power; the priest lives upon sins; it is necessary to him that
there be "sinning."

Friedrich W. Nietzsche

Take off the strong cord of discipline and morality, and you
will be an old man before your twenties are past. Preserve
these forces. Do not burn them out in idleness or crime.

James A. Garfield

You cannot make yourself feel something you do not feel, but
you can make yourself do right in spite of your feelings.

Pearl S. Buck

The secret of all success is to know how to deny yourself.
Prove that you can control yourself, and you are an educated
man; and without this all other education is good for nothing.

R. D. Hitchcock

Deliver yourself from the fetters of lust and passion. . .for God did not create you to be their captive, but that they should be your thralls, under your control, for the journey which is before you.

Al-Ghazzali

Conquer thyself. Till thou hast done this, thou art but a slave; for it is almost as well to be subjected to another's appetite as to thine own.

Richard Burton

Of two evils, pass up the first, and turn down the other.

Anonymous

Doubt

Anxiety is the psychological condition which precedes sin. It is so near, so fearfully near to sin, and yet it is not the explanation of sin.

Søren Kierkegaard

Anxiety is the internal precondition of sin.

Reinhold Niebuhr

There is a deep sickness which infects the soul of modern man. Among rationalists its name is positivism. Among the romantics, its name is existentialism. Both are afraid of life. Both . . . are afraid of reason. Both . . . are afraid of emotion. Neither one has a belief, a hope.

Robert E. Fitch

Every temptation, every tribulation is not deadly. But their multiplicity disorders us, discomposes us, unsettles us, and so hazards us.

John Donne

The devil divides the world between atheism and superstition.

George Herbert

The soul which does not live in God is the author of its own evil; that is why it sins.

Saint Ambrose

Our will is always for our own good, but we do not always see what that is.

Jean-Jacques Rousseau

We look for good on earth and cannot recognize it when met.

Euripides

62

Since Christ from sin us to release
  Hath suffered all this pain,
Why do we not from sin then cease,
  But still in sin remain?

Anonymous

Duty

To be individually righteous is the first of all duties, come what may to one's self, to one's country, to society, and to civilization itself.

Joseph W. Krutch

Every time a Christian cheats on his income tax, he perverts and obscures the Gospel.

John Sanderson

Do not be too moral. You may cheat yourself out of much life. . . . Aim above morality. Be not simply good; be good for something.

Henry David Thoreau

Non-cooperation with evil is as much a duty as is cooperation with good.

Mohandas Gandhi

The only immorality is to not do what one has to do when one has to do it.

Jean Anouilh

Forgive us for bypassing political duties; for condemning civil disobedience when we will not obey You; for reducing Your holy law to average virtues, by trying to be no better or worse than most men.

United Presbyterian Church

It is a duty to say what should be heard, and a duty not to say what should not be heard.

The Talmud

Whoever can pray on behalf of his neighbor and fails to do so is a sinner.

The Talmud

The son pays the father's debts.

Anonymous

Sin is the refusal of the creature to his God who invites him to union with Him.

Columba Marmion

The worse evil of all is to leave the ranks of the living before one dies.

Seneca

E

Envy

Evil

Excuses

Envy

Envy is uneasiness of the mind, caused by the consideration of a good we desire, obtained by one we think should not have it before us.

John Locke

Envy is a coal come hissing hot from hell.

Philip J. Bailey

Envy, the meanest of vices, creeps on the ground like a serpent.

Ovid

Envy shooteth at others and woundeth herself.

Thomas Fuller

Envy is the most corroding of the vices, and also the greatest power in any land.

James M. Barrie

Every other sin hath some pleasure annexed to it, or will admit of an excuse: envy alone wants both.

Robert Burton

There is not a passion so strongly rooted in the human heart
as envy.

Richard Brinsley Sheridan

The envious will die, but envy never.

Molière

Moral indignation is jealousy with a halo.

H.G. Wells

Jealousy is the greatest evil of all, and the one which excites
the least pity in the persons who occasion it.

La Rochefoucauld

What heart-breaking torments from jealousy flow,
Ah! none but the jealous—the jealous can know!

Richard Brinsley Sheridan

An envious man is a squinty-eyed fool.

Henry G. Bohn

I would rather that my enemies envy me than that I should
envy my enemies.

Plautus

Where envying and strife is, there is confusion and every evil
work.

The Bible

As iron is eaten away by rust, so the envious are consumed by
their own passion.

Antisthenes

Expect not praise without envy until you are dead.

Charles C. Colton

Fret not thyself because of evil men, neither be thou envious
at the wicked.

The Bible

Evil

The more deeply we become aware of the reality of evil, the
less we can explain it. Sin is something which we cannot
explain, something which will not fit into any reasonable
scheme at all. For it is the primal fact of non-reason. The
more we try to explain evil, the more we deny its reality, and
the more superficial we become. The more anyone knows
what evil is, the more inexplicable it becomes.

Emil Brunner

Thanks to those gifts which the Creator has given him, man can emancipate himself from his Creator and make himself his own lord. That is what the Bible calls sin. We see at once that this has nothing to do with the animal nature, but has a purely spiritual origin. Evil, understood like this, is much more dangerous, much more profound and alarming, than what idealistic philosophy conceives as evil.

Emil Brunner

We do not need artificially to conjure up a sense of sin. All we need to do is to open our eyes to facts. Take one swift glance at the social state of the world today. . . .That should be sufficient to indicate that this is no fool-proof universe automatically progressive but that moral evil is still the central problem of mankind.

Harry E. Fosdick

Most newspaper headlines are more effective examples of man's sin writ large than any book on theology can ever hope to be.

Robert McAfee Brown

Man is lucky that during childhood he cannot tell good from evil, for if he had mature powers of perception he would die of grief.

Bahya ben Joseph ibn Pakuda

Happy are those who have never tasted evil.

Sophocles

It is tempting to deny the existence of evil, since denying it
obviates the need to fight it.

Alexis Carrel

Destroy the seed of evil, or it will grow up to your ruin.

Aesop

We cannot love good, if we do not hate evil.

Saint Jerome

Woe unto them that call evil good, and good evil.

The Bible

Whoso rewardeth evil for good, evil shall not depart from his
house.

The Bible

Few people know how to liberate themselves from evil.

Pythagoras

Evil is neither suffering nor sin; it is both at the same time, it is
something common to them both. For they are linked together; sin makes us suffer and suffering makes us evil, and
this indissoluble complex of suffering and sin is the evil in
which we are submerged against our will, and to our horror.

Simone Weil

In the face of evil there are three kinds of souls: There are those who do evil and deny that there is evil and call it good. "Yea, the time cometh, that whosoever killeth you will think he doeth God service" (the Bible). There are also those who see evil in others, but not in themselves, and who flatter their own "virtue" by critizing the sinful. "Thou hypocrite, first cast out the beam out of thine own eye; and then shalt thou see clearly to cast out the mote out of thy brother's eye" (the Bible). Finally, there are those who carry the burden of another's woe and sin as their own.

Fulton J. Sheen

Evil springs up, and flowers, and bears no seed,
And feeds the green earth with its swift decay,
Leaving it richer for the growth of truth.

James Russell Lowell

Selfishness is the root and source of all natural and moral evils.

Nathanael Emmons

Evil is easy, its forms are infinite; good is almost unique.

Blaise Pascal

All evils are equal when they are extreme.

Pierre Corneille

Evil is a disrupter and a disease of the soul.

Plato

Evil is whatever does harm.

French proverb

Evil never dies.

Sophocles

Excuses

The true way out is to face up to shame and realize that we can be accepted by God because we are unfit and that we can be pardoned because we are guilty. It is the excuses which spoil us. . . . We are blind to our own faults. That is why we say we need courage to sit down and to ask ourselves whether what we are doing is right or wrong.

Fulton J. Sheen

We are all exceptional cases. . . .Each man insists on being innocent, even if it means accusing the whole human race, and heaven.

Albert Camus

Every vice has its excuse ready.

Publilius Syrus

The most miserable pettifogging in the world is that of a man in the court of his own conscience.

Henry Ward Beecher

We may not sin in order to prevent another's sinning.

Saint Augustine of Hippo

We don't call it sin today—we call it self-expression.

Baroness Stocks

There is a type of person who doesn't go to church because he has sinned. In Christ's estimation that is the person who has one added reason for being in church.

Sebastian Miklas

When the soul is troubled, lonely and darkened, then it turns easily to the outer comfort and to the empty enjoyment of the world.

Saint Francis of Assisi

What is morality in any given time or place? It is what the majority then and there happen to like and immorality is what they dislike.

Alfred North Whitehead

Whoever excuses a sin on the ground of custom could by that same argument excuse any sin.

Jan Hus

Nor custom, nor example, nor vast numbers
Of such as do offend, make less the sin.

Philip Massinger

You are asked to get rid of your sins, not show that others
have committed the like.

Saint John Chrysostom

Right is right, even if everyone is against it; and wrong is
wrong, even if everyone is for it.

William Penn

F

Falling From Grace
Fear
Forbidden Fruits
Forgiveness

Falling From Grace

No one is cast into the abyss unless he has first rejected, freed his heart from the terrible, yet gentle, hand of God. No one is abandoned unless he has first committed the fundamental sacrilege and denied God not in his justice but in his love.

George S. Bernanos

We are surprised at falling: an evident mark that we scarcely know ourselves. We ought, on the contrary, to be surprised at not falling more frequently, and into more grievous faults.

Saint Francis of Sales

For if we never fell, we should not know how feeble and how wretched we are of ourself, and also we should not fully know that marvellous love of our Maker.

Mother Julian of Norwich

Alienation from self and from one's fellow men has its roots in separation from God. Once the hub of the wheel, which is God, is lost, the spokes, which are men, fall apart.

Fulton J. Sheen

He who, leaving virtue, ceaseth to be a man, since he cannot be a partaker of the divine condition, is turned into a beast.

Boethius

It does not matter how small the sins are provided their cumulative effect is to edge the man away from the Light and out into the Nothing. Murder is no better than cards if cards can do the trick.

C. S. Lewis

To act against our conscience is neither safe for us, or open to us.

Martin Luther

Young liars turn into old thieves.

Hebrew proverb

When you get God pulling one way, and the devil the other, each having his feet well braced,—to say nothing of the conscience sawing transversely,—almost any timber will give way.

Henry David Thoreau

I will say it boldly, though God can do all things, He cannot raise a virgin up after she has fallen.

Saint Jerome

To fall into sin is human, but to remain in sin is devilish.

German proverb

Your wickedness makes you, as it were, heavy as lead, and to tend downwards with great weight and pressure towards Hell; and if God should let you go, you would immediately sink and swiftly descend and plunge into the bottomless gulf, and your healthy constitution, and your own care and prudence, and best constrivance, and all your righteousness, would have no more influence to uphold you and keep you out of Hell than a spider's web would have to stop a falling rock.

Jonathan Edwards

The soul accustomed to light transgressions has no horror of more serious ones.

Saint Gregory The Great

Man-like is it to fall into sin,
Fiend-like is it to dwell therein,
Christ-like is it for sin to grieve,
God-like is it all sin to leave.

Friedrich Von Logau

Man's shame is between his legs, a fool's between his cheeks.
Moses ibn Ezra

To be a saint is the exception; to be upright is the rule. Err, falter, sin, but be upright. To commit the least possible sin is the law for man. Sin is a gravitation.

Victor Hugo

Fear

They who feel guilty are afraid, and they who are afraid somehow feel guilty. To the onlooker, too, the fearful seem guilty.

Eric Hoffer

The wicked man travaileth with pain all his days, . . . Trouble and anguish shall make him afraid.

The Bible

Shame arises from the fear of man; conscience from the fear of God.

Samuel Johnson

The wicked flee when no man pursueth: but the righteous are bold as a lion.

The Bible

Consider three things, and you will avoid sin: Above you is an all-seeing eye, an all-hearing ear, and a record of all your acts.

Saying of the Fathers

A brave man hazards life, but not his conscience.

Johann C. F. von Schiller

Evils in the journey of life are like the bells which alarm travellers upon their road; they both appear great at a distance, but when we approach them we find that they are far less insurmountable than we had conceived.

Charles C. Colton

Conscience does make cowards of us all.

Shakespeare

When they are in trouble, the wicked repent; once the trouble is over, they return to their evil ways.

Midrash

Though a sinner do evil a hundred times, and his days be prolonged, yet surely I know that it shall be well with them that fear God.

The Bible

The man who has knowledge but no fear of sin is like a carpenter without tools.

Abot de Rabbi Nathan

When we yield to the fear of evil, we already experience the evil of fear.

Pierre de Beaumarchais

Forbidden Fruits

In order to sin and become culpable in the sight of God, it is necessary to know that the thing we wish to do is not good, or at least to doubt that it is; to fear or to judge that God takes no pleasure in the action which we contemplate, but forbids it; and inspite of this, to commit the deed, leap the fence, and transgress.

Etienne Baumy

When man says "Yes" to the forbidden fruit, he says "No" to the prohibiting God. . . . He estranges himself from God and divine will: aversion to God and the intimate essence of grave sin consist in this.

Pope Pius XII

More men abstain from forbidden actions because they are ashamed of sinning, than because their inclinations are good.

Seneca

Things forbidden have a secret charm.

Tacitus

As long as the evil deed does not bear fruit, the fool thinks it like honey; but when it ripens, then the fool suffers grief.

Subhadra Bhikshu

Adam was but human—this explains it all. He did not want the apple for the apple's sake; he wanted it only because it was forbidden. The mistake was in not forbidding the serpent; then he would have eaten the serpent.

Mark Twain (Samuel Clemens)

There is more fear than delight in a secret pleasure.

Publilius Syrus

He who does not forbid sin when he can, encourages it.

Seneca

Unless the reformer can invent something which substitutes attractive virtues for attractive vices, he will fail.

Walter Lippmann

The only way to get rid of a temptation is to yield to it. Resist it, and your soul grows sick with longing for the things it has forbidden to itself.

Oscar Wilde

We always long for forbidden things, and desire what is denied us.

Rabelais

Stolen waters are sweet, and bread eaten in secret is pleasant.

The Bible

Sin is not hurtful because it is forbidden, but sin is forbidden because it is hurtful.

Benjamin Franklin

Forgiveness

God loves me even while I sin. But it cannot be said too strongly that there is a wrath of God against me as sinning; God's will is set one way and mine is set against it. And therefore, though he longs to forgive, he cannot do so unless either my will is turned from its sinful direction into conformity with his, or else there is at work some power which is capable of effecting that change in me.

William Temple

Forgive us our debts, as we forgive our debtors.

The Bible

Marriage is three parts love and seven parts forgiveness of sins.

Langdon Mitchell

Let the wicked forsake his way, and the unrighteous man his thoughts: and let him return unto the Lord, and he will have mercy upon him; and to our God, for he will abundantly pardon.

The Bible

I will cleanse them from all their iniquity, whereby they have
sinned against me; and I will pardon all their iniquities,
whereby they have sinned, and whereby they have trans-
gressed against me.

The Bible

If God were not willing to forgive sin
Heaven would be empty.

German proverb

The sin which he hath done shall be forgiven him.

The Bible

Charity shall cover the multitude of sins.

The Bible

Sins cannot be undone, only forgiven.

Igor Stravinsky

It is the confession, not the priest, that gives us absolution.

Oscar Wilde

Neither do I condemn thee: go, and sin no more.

The Bible

The one thing that cannot be forgiven is the sin of choosing to be evil, of refusing deliverance. It is impossible to forgive that.

George Macdonald

How can we tell when a sin we have committed has been pardoned? By the fact that we no longer commit that sin.

Rabbi Bunam of Pzysha

G

Gardens of Eden
Good and Evil
Good Intentions
Goodness
Goodness Triumphs
Good Works
Grace
Greed
Guilt

Gardens of Eden

A man's good deeds are used by the Lord as seeds for plant-
ing trees in the Garden of Eden: thus, each man creates his
own Paradise.

The Mezeritzer Rabbi

Why did God create only one man? So that no one could say
virtue and vice are hereditary.

The Talmud

With the first sin came sin into the world. Exactly in the same
way is this true of every subsequent first sin of man, that with
it sin comes into the world.

Søren Kierkegaard

Sin is that inborn corruption of man, derived and propagated
from our first parents, whereby we are immersed in depraved
lusts, averse to goodness and prone to all evil, and unable
of ourselves to do or think anything that is good . . . . We are
all by nature under the Wrath of God, and subject to just
punishment.

Heinrich Bullinger

Sin we have explain'd away;
Unluckily, the sinners stay.

William Allingham

Men will play large sums to whores
For telling them they are not bores.

W. H. Auden

The Devil enters the prompter's box and the play is ready to start.

Robert W. Service

Good and Evil

There is no good without ill in the world,
But everything is mixed in due proportion.

Euripides

There is no evil in human affairs that has not some good mingled with it.

Francesco Guicciardini

He that lacks time to mourn, lacks time to mend.

Henry Taylor

In every rank and condition of life the very bad is mixed with the very good.

Saint Jerome

Good and evil . . . are not what vulgar opinion accounts
them; many who seem to be struggling with adversity are
happy; many, amid great affluence, are utterly miserable.

Tacitus

The world loves a spice of wickedness.

Henry Wadsworth Longfellow

For there is not a just man upon earth, that doeth good, and
sinneth not.

The Bible

Virtue and vice, evil and good, are siblings, or next-door
neighbors. Easy to make mistakes, hard to tell them apart.

Ovid

All things are mixed, the useful with the vain,
The good with bad, the noble with the vile.

Francis Quarles

There's a little bit of the whore in all of us.

Kerry Packer

God himself would not permit evil in this world if good did
not come of it for the benefit and harmony of the universe.

Saint Thomas Aquinas

A good man out of the good treasure of the heart bringeth
forth good things: and an evil man out of the evil treasure
bringeth forth evil things.

> The Bible

The world is all the richer for having the devil in it, so long as
we keep our foot upon his neck.

> William James

Little progress can be made by merely attempting to repress
what is evil; our great hope lies in developing what is good.

> Calvin Coolidge

Goodness and nobility have an inherent power to attract,
whereas self-seeking and evil inevitably repel.

> Francis B. Sayre

The tongue of the just is as choice silver: the heart of the
wicked is little worth.

> The Bible

This only have I found, that God hath made man upright; but
they have sought out many inventions.

> The Bible

Nothing is good for him for whom nothing is bad.

> Baltasar Gracian

The character of human life, like the character of the human condition, like the character of all life, is "ambiguity", the inseparable mixture of good and evil, the true and false, the creative and destructive forces—both individual and social.

Paul Tillich

The righteous promise little and perform much; the wicked promise much and perform not even a little.

The Talmud

He that is faithful in that which is least is faithful also in much: and he that is unjust in the least is unjust also in much.

The Bible

All things have I seen in the days of my vanity: there is a just man that perisheth in his righteousness, and there is a wicked man that prolongeth his life in his wickedness.

The Bible

Good Intentions

All the ways of a man are clean in his own eyes; but the Lord weigheth the spirits.

The Bible

I am often struck by the word Jesus used for sin. It comes from archery practice; to sin (in the thought of Jesus) means to miss the mark: miss the target. To miss the target at least implies you are aiming at something.

G. F. Macleod

———

The heart of virtue is good intentions.

The Talmud

———

The larger part of goodness is the will to become good.

Seneca

———

If better were within, better would come out.

Thomas Fuller

———

The good hate to sin through love of virtue.

Horace

———

It is better to sin out of good intentions than to conform with evil (greedy) intent.

The Talmud

———

Men never do evil so fully and so happily as when they do it for conscience' sake.

Blaise Pascal

That which we call sin in others is experiment for us.

Ralph Waldo Emerson

One must either be good, or imitate a good man.

Democritus of Abdera

Be always sure you are right—then go ahead.

David Crockett

If you set your mind on humanity, you will be free from evil.

Confucius

He does not sin who sins without intent.

Seneca

Goodness

I have met so many good people that I have almost lost my faith in the wickedness of mankind.

Will Durant

Humility, liberality, chastity, meekness, temperance, brotherly love, and diligence, are the virtues contrary to the Seven Capital Sins.

John McCaffrey

That man is good or evil is not indifferent to God; no! He has a lively, profound interest in man's being good; he wills that man should be good, happy—for without goodness there is no happiness.

Ludwig Feuerbach

Many people would be much better if they would let themselves be as good as they really are. They seem to take delight in making themselves less.

Mark Rutherford

The good is, like nature, an immense landscape in which man advances through centuries of exploration.

José Ortega Y Gasset

Sin writes histories, goodness is silent.

Johann W. von Goethe

Beauty, Good, and Knowledge are three sisters;
That doat upon each other, friends to man;
Living together under the same roof,
And never can be sundered without tears.

Alfred Lord Tennyson

The meaning of good and bad, of better and worse, is simply helping or hurting.

Ralph Waldo Emerson

Whatsoever things are true, whatsoever things are honest, whatsoever things are just, whatsoever things are pure, whatsoever things are lovely, whatsoever things are of good report; if there be any virtue, and if there be any praise, think of these things.

The Bible

The modern world is witnessing the liquidation of the idea of the natural goodness of man.

Bishop Fulton J. Sheen

What is good is never plentiful.

Cervantes

Be good and you will be lonesome.

Mark Twain (Samuel Clemens)

Goodness Triumphs

Be good and leave the rest to Heaven.

William Combe

The wicked are always surprised to find that the good can be clever.

Luc de Clapiers de Vauvenargues

He that is good is free, though he be a slave, he that is evil is a slave, though he be a king.

Saint Augustine of Hippo

Be good yourself and the world will be good.

Hindu proverb

When the wicked are multiplied, transgression increaseth: but the righteous shall see their fall.

The Bible

As the whirlwind passeth, so is the wicked no more: but the righteous is an everlasting foundation.

The Bible

Knowest thou not this of old, since man was placed upon earth, that the triumphing of the wicked is short?

The Bible

Virtue is bold, and goodness never fearful.

Shakespeare

There is never an instant's truce between virtue and vice. Goodness is the only investment that never fails.

Henry David Thoreau

The kingdom of heaven is not the isolation of good from evil.
It is the overcoming of evil by good. God has in his nature the
knowledge of evil, of pain, and of degradation, but it is there
as overcome with what is good.

Alfred North Whitehead

How indestructibly the Good grows, and propagates itself,
even among the weedy entanglements of Evil!

Thomas Carlyle

The good hate sin from an innate love of virtue.

Horace

Goodness is simple; badness is manifold.

Aristotle

The good must merit God's peculiar care;
But who but God can tell us who they are?

Alexander Pope

Grant that he may have power and strength to have victory,
and to triumph, against the devil, the world, and the flesh.
Amen.

Book of Common Prayer

Two opposing mysteries are in the world—goodness and evil. If we deny God, then goodness is a mystery, for no one has ever suggested how spiritual life could rise of an unspiritual source, how souls could come from dust. If we affirm God, then evil is a mystery, for why, we ask, should love create a world with so much pain and sin? Our task is not to solve insoluble problems. It is to balance these alternatives—no God and the mystery of man's spiritual life, against God and the mystery of evil.

Harry E. Fosdick

Evil is a reality, and deserves only to be fought. But the means are given to do this. For there is a Power for good that works not only side by side with man, but also in him and through him, flowering in that Freedom which is given to his reason to get at truth, to his emotions, to love the beautiful, the good, and the true, and detest the ugly, the evil, and the false, and to his will and manhood to engage in the struggle.

Edward G. Spaulding

When thou attackest the roots of sin, fix thy thought more upon the God who thou desirest than upon the sin which thou abhorrest.

Walter Hylton

Good Works

Let a good man do good deeds with the same zeal that the evil man docs bad ones.

The Belzer Rabbi

We have to carry on the struggle against the evil that is in mankind, not by judging others, but by judging ourselves. Struggle with oneself and veracity towards oneself are the means by which we influence others. We quietly draw them into our efforts to attain the deep spiritual self-realization which springs from reverence for one's own life.

Albert Schweitzer

Happiness is not best achieved by those who seek it directly; and it would seem that the same is true of the good.

Bertrand Russell

Virtue must shape itself in deed.

Alfred Lord Tennyson

Break off thy sins by righteousness.

The Bible

In doing good we are generally cold, and languid, and sluggish; and of all things afraid of being too much in the right. But the works of malice and injustice are quite in another style. They are finished with a bold masterly hand.

Edmund Burke

You don't make up for your sins in church. You do it at home and you do it in the streets.

Martin Sorsese

Fight with your own sin, and let that fight keep you humble and full of sympathy when you go out into the world and strike at the sin of which the world is full. Fight with the world's sin, and let the needs of that fight make you aware of how much is wrong, and make you eager that everything shall be right within yourself.

Phillips Brooks

More men become good through practice than by nature.

Democritus of Abdera

God is better served in resisting a temptation to evil than in many formal prayers.

William Penn

It is good to be tired and wearied by the vain search after the true good, that we may stretch out our arms to the Redeemer.

Blaise Pascal

It's so much easier to do good than to be good.

Bertie C. Forbes

Grace

Grace is unconquerable love. . .waits not for merit to call it forth, but flows out to the most guilty, is the sinner's only hope.

William Ellery Channing

The measure of God's anger against sin is the measure of the love that is prepared to forgive the sinner and to love him in spite of his sin.

David M. Lloyd-Jones

He maketh his sun to rise on the evil and on the good, and sendeth rain on the just and on the unjust.

The Bible

If we confess our sins, he is faithful and just to forgive us our sins, and to cleanse us from all unrighteousness.

The Bible

Man does not commit a sin unless he is possessed by folly.

The Talmud

He that falls into sin is a man; that grieves at it, is a saint; that boasteth of it, is a devil.

Thomas Fuller

Thus saith the Lord, Let not the wise man glory in his wisdom, neither let the mighty man glory in his might, let not the rich man glory in his riches: but let him that glorieth glory in this, that he understandeth and knoweth me, that I am the Lord which exercise loving-kindness, judgment, and righteousness, in the earth: for in these things I delight, saith the Lord.

The Bible

Sin is the disease. Christ the cure. The result is miracle.
Frank N. D. Buchman

Sin is sovereign till sovereign grace dethrones it.
Charles H. Spurgeon

Greed

O Lord, the sin
Done for the things there's money in.
John Edward Masefield

For the love of money is the root of all evil: which while some coveted after, they have erred from the faith, and pierced themselves through with many sorrows. But thou, o man of God, flee these things; and follow after righteousness, godliness, faith, love, patience, meekness.
The Bible

To possess money is very well; to be possessed by it is to be possessed by a devil.
Tryon Edwards

A great evil is the number of people who are trying to get something for nothing, and a greater evil is the number of people who succeed.
Anonymous

To the covetous man life is a nightmare, and God lets him
wrestle with it as best he may.

Henry Ward Beecher

Avarice, in wanting to gain everything, loses all.

Jean de La Fontaine

Excess of wealth is cause of covetousness.

Christopher Marlowe

Covetousness, as denoting a special sin, is called the root of
all sins, in likeness to the root of a tree, in furnishing suste-
nance to the whole tree. For we see that by riches man
acquires the means of committing any sin whatever, and of
sating his desire for any sin whatever, since money helps man
to obtain all manner of temporal goods. . . . So that in this
sense desire for riches is the root of all sins.

Saint Thomas Aquinas

To the cynic, money isn't the root of all evil—evil is the root of
all money.

Anonymous

Morals today are corrupted by our worship of riches.

Cicero

Love of money is the root of half the evil in the world, and lack of money is the root of the other half.

Anonymous

All things, divine and human—virtue, fame, honor—are slaves to the beauty of riches.

Horace

Long after all other sins are old, avarice remains young.

French proverb

Guilt

This is the first punishment, that by the verdict of his own heart no guilty man is acquitted.

Juvenal

He declares himself guilty who justifies himself before accusation.

Thomas Fuller

Without the spice of guilt, sin cannot be fully savored.

Alexander Chase

The wages of sin are in the sin itself.

Michel Servin

Guilt itself is a desirable human emotion in the sense that it enables us to recognize what we have done wrong, when we have violated our own consciences and the mores of society.
Sidney M. Jourard

A sense of wrongdoing is an enhancement of pleasure.
Oliver Wendell Holmes

Multitudes think they like to do evil; yet no man ever really enjoyed doing evil since God made the world.
John Ruskin

A scar on the conscience is the same as a wound.
Publilius Syrus

It is against himself that everybody sins.
Latin proverb

The chief and greatest punishment for sin is the fact of having sinned.
Seneca

As virtue is its own reward, so vice is its own punishment.
Thomas Fuller

H

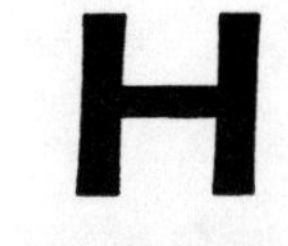

Hate

Honesty

Honor

Humility

Hypocrisy

Hate

All anger is not sinful, because some degree of it, and on some occasions, is inevitable. But it becomes sinful and contradicts the rule of Scripture when it is conceived upon slight and inadequate provocation, and when it continues long.

William Paley

Hating people is like burning down your own house to get rid of a rat.

Harry E. Fosdick

The continuance of anger is hatred.

Frances Quarles

The easiest thing in the world is malice.

Laurence Harvey

An angry tongue is worse than a wicked hand.

Hebrew proverb

Nothing that a man does takes him lower than when he allows himself to fall so far as to hate anyone.

Martin Luther King, Sr.

Well, this is what we must overcome first of all. Our poisoned hearts must be cured. And the most difficult battle to be won against the enemy in the future must be fought within ourselves, with an exceptional effort that will transform our appetite for hatred into a desire for justice.

Albert Camus

It is a sin peculiar to man to hate his victim.

Tacitus

These two sins, hatred and pride, deck and trim themselves out as the devil clothed himself in the Godhead. Hatred will be godlike; pride will be truth. These two are deadly sins: hatred is killing, pride is lying.

Martin Luther

There is no medicine to cure hatred.

African proverb

There would be no place for hatred among wise men. For who but the foolish would hate good men? And there is no cause to hate bad men. Vice is a disease of the mind, just as feebleness shows ill health to the body.

Boethius

Our hatred of someone does not affect their peace of mind, but it certainly can ruin ours.

W. A. Nance

The price of hating other human beings is loving oneself less.
Eldridge Cleaver

Honesty

There is a difference between telling a falsehood and lying. One who lies is not himself deceived, but tries to deceive another; he who tells a falsehood is himself deceived. One who lies deceives, as far as he is able; but one who tells a falsehood does not himself deceive, any more than he can help. A good man ought to take pains not to lie; a wise man, not to tell what is false.
Publius Nigidius

It takes a wise man to handle a lie; a fool had better remain honest.
Norman Douglas

For thirteen years I taught my tongue not to tell a lie; for the next thirteen, I taught it to tell the truth.
The Koretser Rabbi

The lip of truth shall be established for ever: but a lying tongue is but for a moment.
The Bible

Let not mercy and truth forsake thee: bind them about thy neck; write them upon the table of thine heart.
The Bible

Honesty is the best policy because it has so little competition.
Arnold Glasow

Honesty is the best policy; but he who is governed by that maxim is not an honest man.
Richard Whately

Honesty isn't any policy at all; it's a state of mind or it isn't honesty.
Eugene L'Hote

I have not observed men's honesty to increase with their riches.
Thomas Jefferson

Honor

A man who permits his honor to be taken, permits his life to be taken.
Pietro Aretino

Honor is like a steep island without a shore: one cannot return once one is outside.

Nicolas Boileau

―――

A man of honor should never forget what he is because he sees what others are.

Baltasar Gracian

―――

Even honor and virtue make enemies, condemning, as they do, their opposites by too close a contrast.

Tacitus

―――

Honour and shame from no condition rise;
Act well your part, there all the honour lies.

Alexander Pope

―――

Morality regulates the acts of man as a private individual; honor, his acts as a public man.

Esteban Echeverria

―――

He has honor if he holds himself to an ideal of conduct though it is inconvenient, unprofitable, or dangerous to do so.

Walter Lippmann

Hold it the greatest wrong to prefer life to honor and for the sake of life to lose the reason for living.

Juvenal

If it seems to me that he has not attained to virtue, and yet asserts that he has, I will reproach him for holding cheapest what is worth most, and dearer what is worth less. This I will do for old and young,—for every man I meet. . . .

Plato

When faith is lost, when honor dies,
The man is dead.

John Greenleaf Whittier

Humility

The less a man thinks or knows about his virtues, the better we like him.

Ralph Waldo Emerson

To be proud of virtue is to poison yourself with the antidote.

Benjamin Franklin

If you conceal your vices, conceal your virtues.

Ibn Zabara

Each of us when he appears before his fellows is clothed in a certain dignity. But every man knows what unconfessable things pass within the secrecy of his own heart.

Luigi Pirandello

Man's finest virtue is that of which he is unaware.

Shirat Yisrael

Every day we plead in the Lord's Prayer,
"Thy will be done!" yet when His will is done
We grumble and are not pleased with it.

Meister Eckhart (Johannes)

God is everywhere, even in evil thoughts.

Hebrew proverb

If you would be good, first believe that you are bad.

Epictetus

When thinking of sinners we shall never go wrong to include ourselves.

Aelred Graham

Hypocrisy

Better to be known as a sinner than a hypocrite.

Danish proverb

To be always intending to live a new life, but never to find time to set about it; this is as if a man put off eating and drinking and sleeping from one day and night to another, till he starved and destroyed.

John Tillotson

Beware of the pious fool, and the wise sinner.

Solomon ben Yehuda ibn Gabirol

Of all villainy, there is none more base than that of the hypocrite, who, at the moment he is most false, takes care to appear most virtuous.

Cicero

Be not too hasty to trust or admire the teachers of morality; they discourse like angels, but they live like men.

Samuel Johnson

I hope you have not been leading a double life, pretending to be wicked and being really good all the time. That would be hypocrisy.

Oscar Wilde

Men, said the Devil, are good to their brothers: they don't
want to mend their own ways but each other's.

Piet Hein

Any of us can achieve virtue, if by virtue we merely mean the
avoidance of the vices that do not attract us.

Robert S. Lynd

Evil is a hill, every one gets on his own and speaks about
someone else's.

African proverb

If we say that we have no sin, we deceive ourselves, and the
truth is not in us.

The Bible

If people fought sin as hard as they do middle age, earth
would be a moral paradise.

Hal Boyle

Hypocrisy is the homage which vice pays to virtue.

La Rochefoucauld

Indulgent gods, grant me to sin once with impunity. That is
sufficient. Let a second offense bear its punishment.

Ovid

I

Idle Hands
In God's Image
In High Places
Innocence
Integrity
Its Own Reward

Idle Hands

From its very inaction, idleness ultimately becomes the most active cause of evil; as a palsy is more to be dreaded than a fever. The Turks have a proverb which says that the devil tempts all other men, but that idle men tempt the devil.

Charles C. Colton

If thou hast nothing to do, thou shalt be haled in pieces with envy, lust, some passion or other.

Robert Burton

A man is never alone, not only because he is with himself and his own thoughts, but because he is with the Devil, who ever consorts with our solitude.

Thomas Browne

Solitude is the playfield of Satan.

Vladimir Nabokov

Idleness is the ruin of chastity.

Latin proverb

The longer thread of life we spin,
The more occasion still to sin.

Robert Herrick

Temptation rarely comes in working hours. It is in their leisure time that men are made or marred.

W. M. Taylor

The devil never tempted a man whom he found judiciously employed.

Charles H. Spurgeon

Idleness, n. A model farm where the devil experiments with seeds of new sins and promotes the growth of staple vices.

Ambrose Bierce

Idleness: the nurse of sin.

Edmund Spenser

In God's Image

Whence come my conceptions of the intelligence, and justice, and goodness, and power of God? It is because my own spirit contains the germs of these attributes.

William Ellery Channing

Sin is the infidelity of man to the image of what he ought to be in his eternal vocation as an adapted son of God.

Fulton J. Sheen

Basically, man is good, not bad; or he would not feel remorse and he would not repent when the good in him has been temporarily defeated.

Jay W. Hudson

There are sparks of holiness in everything; they constitute our spirituality.

The Mezeritzer Rabbi

Conscience is God's presence in Man.

Emanuel Swedenborg

Sin is no part of the true constitution of any member of the human race.

Evelyn Frost

Under all the false, overloaded and glittering masquerade, there is in every man a noble nature beneath.

Berthold Auerbach (Theobald Chauber)

Man is not born wicked: he becomes so, as he becomes sick.

Voltaire

There is not only good in man but also evil, just as there is not only truth in the world but also falsehood. Man's finite endeavors may be swayed by the influence of evil, and his finite intellect may fall prey to the lures of falsehood. But though he be susceptible to evil and error—for inadequacy and finiteness are part of the human condition—man is not evil by nature, that is, not by divine intent. . . .

Herman Cohen

The evil in the world is indeed terrifyingly real, both at the subpersonal and at the personal level; but it is still part of the face of God. That is to say, love is there to be met and to be created through it and out of it.

John A.T. Robinson

There are no incorrigible sinners; God has no permanent problem children.

Nels F. S. Ferre

Instead of telling men they are sinners Vedanta takes the opposite position and says "You are pure and perfect, and what you call sin does not belong to you." Sins are very low degrees of Self-manifestation, manifest the Self in a high degree. That is the one thing to remember.

Swami Vivekananda

In High Places

People like the exposure of wickedness. . . in high places. It gives them a sense of ultimate righteousness of the world. . . the squirming of those who are caught allows people to indulge in a certain legitimate sadism which, otherwise, they would feel obliged to suppress.

John Kenneth Galbraith

The sins of common, untutored people are nothing in comparison with the sins committed by great and high persons, that are in spiritual and temporal offices.

Martin Luther

I have seen the wicked in great power,
and spreading himself like a green bay tree.
Yet he passed away, and, lo, he was not:
yea, I sought him, but he could not be found.

The Bible

Would that the simple maxim, that honesty is the best policy, might be laid to heart; that a sense of the true aim of life might elevate the tone of politics and trade till public and private honor became identical.

Margaret Fuller

It is true that we have not deliberately or wholly abandoned the Christian element in our tradition, but does that element count with us as it once did? Is the moral tone of the nation—its politics, its business life, its literature, its theatre, its movies, its radio networks, its television stations—Christian?

Robert J. McCracken

If a superior man abandon virtue, how can he fulfil the requirements of that name?

Confucius

One of the reasons why sin is so attractive is because it is so well advertised.

Anonymous

One good vice will get you more publicity than a dozen virtues.

Anonymous

He who practices right, but in the hope of acquiring great renown, is very near to vice.

Napoleon Bonaparte

Public virtue cannot exist in a nation without private, and public virtue is the only foundation of republics.

John Adams

It is by its promise of a sense of power that evil often attracts the weak.

Eric Hoffer

Evil men by their own nature cannot ever prosper.

Euripides

The glory that goes with wealth and beauty is fleeting and fragile; virtue is a possession glorious and eternal.

Sallust

Innocence

Blessed is he whose transgression is forgiven,
whose sin is covered.
Blessed is the man unto whom the Lord
  imputeth not iniquity,
in whose spirit there is no guile.

The Bible

Blushing is the color of virtue.

Diogenes the Cynic

Until a child is one year old it is incapable of sin.

The Talmud

Nothing so completely baffles one who is full of trick and duplicity himself, than straightforward and simple integrity in another.

Charles C. Colton

Nature knows no indecencies; man invents them.

Mark Twain (Samuel Clemens)

The only deadly sin I know is cynicism.

Henry L. Stimson

Unless it's right next door, people don't notice killing and bloodshed. We take it in like the sun shines and the rain falls.

Eileen O'Casey

The state of innocence contains the germs of all future sin.

Alexandre Arnoux

Integrity

The courage of all one really knows comes but late in life.

Friedrich W. Nietzsche

Men imagine that they communicate their virtue or vice only by overt actions, and do not see that virtue or vice emit a breath every moment.

Ralph Waldo Emerson

The strength of a man's virtue must not be measured by his efforts, but by his ordinary life.

Blaise Pascal

Good and bad are but names very readily transferable to that or this; the only right is what is after my constitution; the only wrong what is against it.

Ralph Waldo Emerson

The measure of any man's virtue is what he would do, if he had neither the laws nor public opinion, nor even his own prejudices, to control him.

William Hazlitt

It is not only for an exterior show or ostentation that our soul must play her part, but inwardly within ourselves, where no eyes shine but ours.

Montaigne

Any man may play his part in the mummery, and act the honest man on the scaffolding; but to be right within, in his own bosom, where all is allowed, where all is concealed— there's the point! The next step is to be so in our own home, in our ordinary actions, of which we need render no account to any man, where there is no study, no make-believe.

Montaigne

Nothing is at last sacred but the integrity of our own mind. Absolve you to yourself, and you shall have the suffrage of the world.

Ralph Waldo Emerson

Poverty cannot disgrace the wise, nor can lust enslave them.

Ibn Gabirol

The only time a son should disobey his father is if the father orders him to commit a sin.

The Talmud

Integrity without knowledge is weak and useless, and knowledge without integrity is dangerous and dreadful.

Samuel Johnson

This above all: to thine own self be true,
And it must follow, as the night the day,
Thou canst not then be false in any man.

Shakespeare

Its Own Reward

Goodness is the only value that seems in this world of appearances to have any claim to be an end in itself. Virtue is its own reward. I am ashamed to have reached so commonplace a conclusion.

W. Somerset Maugham

Virtue must be valuable, if men and women of all degrees pretend to have it.

Edgar Howe

Virtue, though in rags, will keep me warm.

John Dryden

One trouble with being virtuous is that you can't tell your friends about it afterwards.

Anonymous

I have never seen a man as fond of virtue as of women.

Confucius

Virtue is the roughest way,
But provest at night a bed of down.

Henry Wotton

All sober inquirers after truth, ancient and modern, pagan and Christian, have declared that the happiness of man, as well as his dignity, consists in virtue.

John Adams

One should seek virtue for its own sake, and not from hope or fear, or any external motive. It is in virtue that happiness consists, for virtue is the state of mind which tends to make the whole of life harmonious.

Zeno

As to virtue. . . it is an act of the will, a habit which increases the quantity, intensity and quality of life. It builds up, strengthens and vivifies personality.

Alexis Carrel

Happiness cannot be the reward of virtue; it must be the intelligible consequence of it.

Walter Lippmann

If virtue were its own reward, it would no longer be a human quality, but supernatural.

Luc de Clapiers de Vauvenargues

J

Judging
Judgment Days

Judging

There is perhaps no phenomenon which contains so much destructive feeling as moral indignation, which permits envy or hate to be acted out under the guise of virtue.

Erich Fromm

Men always love what is good or what they find good: it is in judging what is good that they go wrong.

Jean-Jacques Rousseau

Inability to tell good from evil is the greatest worry of man's life.

Cicero

No man better knows what good is than he who hath endureth evil.

John Ray

She that knows sin knows best how to hate sin.

Thomas Middleton

Nothing so needs reforming as other people's habits.

Mark Twain (Samuel Clemens)

Sin . . . has been made not only ugly but passé. People are no longer sinful, they are only immature or underprivileged or frightened or, more particularly, sick.

Phyllis McGinley

We estimate vices and weigh sins not according to their nature, but according to our advantage and self-interest.

Montaigne

See not evil in others and good in yourself, but the good in the other and the failings in yourself.

The Berdichever Rabbi

Conscience is an instinct to judge ourselves in the light of moral laws. It is not a mere faculty; it is an instinct.

Immanuel Kant

He is a truly virtuous man who wishes always to be open to the observation of honest men.

La Rochefoucauld

Ye may put difference between holy and unholy, and between unclean and clean.

The Bible

Judgment Days

Now I've laid me down to die,
I pray my neighbors not to pry
Too deeply into sins that I,
Not only cannot here deny,
But much enjoyed as life flew by.

Preston Sturges

Good and evil are so set, differing from each other just as reward and punishment are in opposition to each other: hence the rewards, which we see fall to the good, must correspond precisely to the punishment of the evil on the side.

Boethius

Even if he should wish to do so, a man could never shake off consience. . . . He will travel along the whole way of his life, and likewise with it, a truthful and incorruptible witness, he will come up for God's judgment.

Pope Pius XII

Thy merry sins, thy laughing sins, shall grow to be crying sins even in the ears of God.

John Donne

Man may securely sin, but safely never.

Ben Jonson

Just as a very little fresh water is blown away by a storm of wind and dust, in like manner the good deeds, that we think we do in this life, are overwhelmed by the multitude of evils.

Saint Basil

When good befalls a man he calls it Providence, when evil Fate.

Knut Hamsun

Know that men suffer under the evils they have brought upon themselves.

Pythagoras

When one has broken the tenth commandment, the others are not of much account.

Mark Twain (Samuel Clemens)

Most people are angry with the sinner, not with the sin.

Seneca

We anger God with our sins, and men with our virtues.

Hebrew proverb

As it is said of the greatest liar that he tells more truth than falsehood, so it may be said of the worst man that he does more good than evil.

Samuel Johnson

When wicked persons have gone on in a course of sin, and find they have reason to fear the just judgment of God for their sins, they begin at first to wish that there were no God to punish them; then by degrees they persuade themselves that there is none; and then they set themselves to study for arguments to back their opinion.

John Bunyan

He that diligently seeketh good procureth favor: but he that seeketh mischief, it shall come unto him.

The Bible

It would be better to eschew sin than to flee from death.

Thomas à Kempis

Let your every act and word and thought be those of a man ready to depart from life this moment.

Marcus Aurelius

The wicked is snared in the work of
   his own hands . . . .
The wicked shall be turned into hell.

The Bible

Prosperous sinners fare worst of all in the end.

Saint John Chrysostom

L

Lesser Evils
Love
Lust
Lying

Lesser Evils

Modern man's loss of a sense of being sinful doesn't spring from a feeling that he is inherently good. Rather, it springs from his feeling of being inherently ineffectual.

Brendan Francis

When choosing between two evils, I always like to take the one I've never tried before.

Mae West

When you choose the lesser of two evils, always remember that it is still an evil.

Max Lerner

Never open the door to a lesser evil, for other and greater ones invariably slink in after it.

Baltasar Gracian

Satan is inconsistent. He persuades a man not to go to synagogue on a cold morning; yet when the man does go, he follows him into it.

The Koretser Rabbi

To prefer evil to good is not in human nature; and when a man is compelled to choose one of two evils, no one will choose the greater when he might have the less.

Plato

If you are standing upright, don't worry if your shadow is crooked.

Chinese proverb

Love

And let no man's sins dishearten thee; love a man even in his sin, for that love is a likeness of the divine love, and is the summit of love on earth.

Father Zossima

The measure of God's anger against sin is the measure of the love that is prepared to forgive the sinner and to love him in spite of his sin.

David M. Lloyd-Jones

Kindness has converted more sinners than zeal, eloquence or learning.

Frederick W. Faber

The monstrosity of sexual intercourse outside marriage is that those who indulge in it are trying to isolate one kind of union (the sexual) from all other kinds of union which were intended to go along with it and make up the total union.

C. S. Lewis

———

As to virtue leading us to a happy life, I hold virtue to be nothing else than perfect love of God.

Saint Augustine of Hippo

———

The first step to Virtue, is to love Virtue in another man.

Thomas Fuller

———

Free love is sometimes love but never freedom.

Elizabeth Bibesco

———

Love grows, Lust wastes by Enjoyment, and Reason is, that one springs from an Union of Souls, and the other from an Union of Sense.

William Penn

———

Where there is love there is no sin.

Montenegrin proverb

———

A minor saint is capable of loving minor sinners. A great saint loves great sinners.

Rabbi Israel Baal-Shem Tob

Lust

A soul, in God's account, is valued at the price of the blood, and shame, and tortures of the Son of God; and yet we throw it away for the exchange of sins that a man is naturally ashamed to own; we lose it for the pleasure, the sottish, beastly pleasure of a night.

Jeremy Taylor

Lust should be stifled, for it cannot lead to truth.

Moses ibn Izra

Lechery . . . is one of the seven deadly sins.

Anonymous

I think only of the joy and forget the folly—I lose sight of common sense, and follow my desire.

Arnaut de Mareuil

Below the navel there is neither religion nor truth.

Italian proverb

From desire I plunge to its fulfilment, where I long once more for desire.

Johann W. von Goethe

In all enjoyment there is a choice between enjoying the other and enjoying yourself through the instrumentality of the other. The first is the enjoyment of love, the second is the enjoyment of lust. When people enjoy themselves through each other, that is merely mutual lust.

John McMurray

What is essentially wrong with lust is not that the body is used carnally but that the situation is such, the human relations are such, that this particular use of the body is the implementation of a wrong spirit.

James A. Pike

The doctors treat venereal disease as a medical problem. Lately they have been calling it a social problem. I say it is a moral problem.

Alvie L. McKnight

Banish all objects of lust, shut up all youth into the severest discipline that can be exercised in any hermitage, ye cannot make them chaste, that came not thither so.

John Milton

Too often the saint has agreed with the debauchee that the only difference between married love and lust is that one is allowed and the other is not.

Sydney Cave

To keep thee from the evil woman, from the flattery of the tongue of a strange woman. Lust not after her beauty in thine heart; neither let her take thee with her eyelids. For by means of a whorish woman a man is brought to a piece of bread: and the adulteress will hunt for the precious life. Can a man take fire in his bosom, and his clothes not be burned? Can one go upon hot coals, and his feet not be burned? So he that goeth in to his neighbor's wife; whosoever toucheth her shall not be innocent.

The Bible

In a maiden, temptation sleeps; in a wife, it's wide awake.

Hebrew proverb

To avoid fornication, let every man have his own wife, and let every woman have her own husband.

The Bible

Lust is like rot in the bones.

Hebrew proverb

From lust comes grief, from lust comes fear; he that is free from lust knows neither grief nor fear.

Dhammapada

Blessed is the man that endureth temptation: for when he is tried, he shall receive the crown of life, which the Lord hath promised to them that love him. Let no man say when he is tempted, I am tempted of God; for God cannot be tempted with evil, neither tempteth he any man: but every man is tempted, when he is drawn away of his own lust, and enticed. Then when lust hath conceived, it bringeth forth sin: and sin, when it is finished, bringeth forth death.

The Bible

Wherefore God also gave them up to uncleanness, through the lusts of their own hearts, to dishonor their own bodies between themselves: who changed the truth of God into a lie, and worshipped and served the creature more than the Creator, who is blessed for ever. Amen.

The Bible

A physical gratification bought at the expense of conscience is the bargain of a fool.

John A. O'Brien

Lying

There are 869 different forms of lying, but only one of them has been squarely forbidden: Thou shalt not bear false witness against thy neighbor.

Mark Twain (Samuel Clemens)

What man is he that desireth life,
and loveth many days, that he may see good?
Keep thy tongue from evil,
and thy lips from speaking guile.

The Bible

Sin has many tools, but a lie is the handle that fits them all.

Oliver Wendell Holmes

Every violation of truth is not only a sort of suicide in the
liar, but is a stab at the health of human society.

Ralph Waldo Emerson

In plain truth, lying is an accursed vice. We are not men, nor
have other tie upon one another, but by our word.

Montaigne

A lie leads a man from a grove into a jungle.

Marcelene Cox

The devil sometimes speaks the truth.

Henry Glapthorne

A liar isn't believed even when he speaks the Truth.

German proverb

Truth is tough. It will not break, like a bubble, at a touch;
nay, you may kick it about all day, like a football, and it will
be round and full at evening.

Oliver Wendell Holmes

The liar's punishment is not in the least that he is not believed
but that he cannot believe anyone else.

George Bernard Shaw

Truth will rise above falsehood as oil above water.

Cervantes

Satan deals with confusion and lies. Put the truth in front of
him and he is gone.

Paul Matlock

Tell the truth and shame the Devil.

François Rabelais

Truth makes the Devil blush.

Thomas Fuller

A little truth helps the lie go down.

Italian proverb

A lie, turned topsy-turvy, can be prinked and tinselled out, decked in plumage new and fine, till none knows its lean old carcass.

Henrik Ibsen

Sure men were born to lie, and women to believe them!

John Gay

Lies can be so furbished and disguised in gorgeous wrappings that not a soul would recognize their skinny carcasses.

Henrik Ibsen

All lies are not told—some are lived.

Arnold Glasow

Mocking God
Moderation
Morality
Motivation

Mocking God

We need a deeper and more tormenting sense of sin, a profounder consciousness of the eternal truth that a sin whether of indifference or intent against our brother or our sister is an offense against an outraged and indignant God.

C. S. MacFarland

Fools make a mock at sin.

The Bible

He who sins against Heaven has nowhere left for prayer.

Confucius

In some sort of crude sense which no vulgarity, no humor, no overstatement can quite extinguish, the physicists have known sin; and this is a knowledge which they cannot lose.

J. Robert Oppenheimer

Who spits against heaven, it falls in his face.

George Herbert

Sin is a reflection upon God.

Benjamin Whichcote

The evil of sin consists in its being the fully wilful rejection of God; it is, as it were, an attempt to annihilate God, and, were this possible, it would do so. . . . It is only in so far as we realize that God is one supreme Reality that we can realize that sin is the one supreme evil.

Bruno Webb

Talk of the devil, and his horns appear, says the proverb.

Samuel T. Coleridge

The devil has nothing to say about the will of God. For he hates this will and categorically refuses to do its bidding. He refuses to stand "under" God. He stands "outside"—as we see—as the cunning observer, the mischief-maker and intriguer.

Helmut Thielicke

When I hate some one or deny that God is my father—it is not he that loses, but me: for then I have no father.

Søren Kierkegaard

The soul which does not live in God is the author of its own evil; that is why it sins.

Saint Ambrose

We must never feel that God will, through some breath-taking miracle or a wave of the hand, cast evil out of the world. As long as we believe this we will pray unanswerable prayers and ask God to do things that he will never do. The belief that God will do everything for a man is as untenable as the belief that man can do everything for himself. It, too, is based on lack of faith.

Martin Luther King, Jr.

If you follow an earthly will, every step you take is a departure from God, till you become as incapable of God and the life of God as the animals of this world.

William Law

If it is an extraordinary blindness to live without investigating what we are, it is a terrible one to live an evil life, while believing in God.

Blaise Pascal

Think not of the smallness of your sin, but of the greatness of Him against whom you have sinned!

Bahya ben Joseph ibn Pakuda

Moderation

Good and bad men are each less so than they seem.

Samuel T. Coleridge

A good is never productive of evil but when it is carried to a culpable excess, in which case it completely ceases to be good.

Voltaire

The extremes of vice and virtue are alike detestable; absolute virtue is as sure to kill a man as absolute vice is.

Samuel Butler

Each virtue in its extreme becomes a vice.

Joseph Ben Hanan Ezobi

Sin may be clasped so close we cannot see its face.

Richard Chenevix Trench

Our errors and our controversies, in the sphere of morality, arise sometimes from looking on men as though they could be altogether bad, or altogether good.

Luc de Clapiers de Vauvenargues

There are people who are virtuous only in a piece-meal way; virtue is a fabric from which they never make themselves a whole garment.

Joseph Joubert

Be not over much wicked, neither be thou foolish: why shouldest thou die before thy time?

The Bible

Morality

Evil becomes an operative motive far more easily than good; but once pure good has become an operative motive in the mind, it forms there the fount of a uniform and inexhaustible impulsion, which is never so in the case of evil.

Simone Weil

Every man takes care that his neighbor shall not cheat him. But a day comes when he begins to care that he does not cheat his neighbor. Then all goes well.

Ralph Waldo Emerson

The whole speculation about morality is an effort to find a way of living which men who live it will instinctively feel is good.

Walter Lippmann

All sects differ, because they come from men; morality is everywhere the same, because it comes from God.

Voltaire

A mental possession of ours which enables us to pass some
sort of judgment, correct or mistaken, upon moral questions
as they arise. . . . your conscience is simply that ideal of life
which constitutes your moral personality.

Josiah Royce

Morality is a private and costly luxury.

Henry Adams

What is moral is what you feel good after and what is immoral
is what you feel bad after.

Ernest Hemingway

Morality is the thing upon which friends smile, and immorality is the thing on which they frown.

Elbert Hubbard

It is not best that we use our morals week days; it gets them
out of repair for Sundays.

Mark Twain (Samuel Clemens)

Too many moralists begin with a dislike of reality.

Clarence Day

A man who moralizes is usually a hypocrite, and a woman
who moralizes is invariably plain.

Oscar Wilde

We all measure good and evil by the pleasure or pain we feel
at present, or expect hereafter.

Thomas Hobbes

If your morals make you dreary, depend on it they are wrong.

Robert Louis Stevenson

You can't straighten what is crooked without a ruler.

Seneca

The only cheap thing around here nowadays is immorality.

Plautus

I lost my moral compass.

Jeb Stuart Magruder

The so-called new morality is too often the old immorality
condoned.

Lord Shawcross

There is an idea abroad among moral people that they should
make their neighbors good. One person I have to make good:
myself.

Robert Louis Stevenson

A man may not transgress the bounds of major morals, but may make errors in minor morals.

Confucius

If there is one thing worse than the modern weakening of major morals it is the modern strengthening of minor morals.

G. K. Chesterton

What we call "morals" is simply blind obedience to words of command.

Havelock Ellis

Compassion is the basis of all morality.

Arthur Schopenhauer

Motivation

When thou attackest the roots of sin, fix thy thought more upon God who thou desirest than upon the sin which thou abhorrest.

Walter Hylton

The word sin in the Bible means something more than the external works done by our bodily action. It means all the circumstances that act together and excite or incite us to what is done; in particular, the impulses operating in the depths of our hearts.

Martin Luther

The sin of the heart is the beginning and, so to speak, the root of all sin; the word and deed that spring from it merely bring it to its full development.

Etienne Gilson

You can put a chastity belt around the body, but you cannot put it around the mind.

Anonymous

The mind sins, not the body; if there is no intention, there is no blame.

Livy

If Satan were to write a book it would be in praise of virtue, because the good would purchase it for use, and the bad for ostentation.

Charles C. Colton

It is funny but true, a man will sin most when he is happiest.
Peggy Hopkins Joyce

Young men want to be faithful, and are not; old men want to
be faithless, and cannot.

Oscar Wilde

═══

The good opinion of our fellow men is the strongest, though
not the purest motive to virtue.

Charles C. Colton

═══

If rascals knew the advantages of virtue they would become
honest men out of rascality.

Benjamin Franklin

═══

When we are happy we are always good, but when we are
good we are not always happy.

Oscar Wilde

═══

Men are less sensible of good than of evil.

Livy

═══

Whoever acts without conscience, or against conscience,
though the very thing he does should be good, sins by doing
it.

Louis Bourdalove

═══

God first looks at a man's heart, then at his mind.

Hebrew proverb

This still small voice (conscience) insistently has called to whatever is best in men and led them on to deeds of uncalculating devotion.

Edmund W. Sinnott

Goodness without wisdom always accomplishes evil.

Robert A. Heinlein

O

Occasions of Sin
Old Time Religion
Original Sin

Occasions of Sin

More and greater sins are committed when people are alone than when they are in society. In solitary places the Devil has opportunity to mislead people. But whosoever is in honest company is ashamed to sin, or at least has no occasion for it.

Martin Luther

Must I do all the evil I can before I learn to shun it? Is it not enough to know the evil to shun it? If not, we should be sincere enough to admit that we love evil too well to give it up.

Mohandas Gandhi

No one can ask honestly or hopefully to be delivered from temptation unless he has himself honestly and firmly determined to do the best he can to keep out of it.

John Ruskin

When there's marriage without love, there will be love without marriage.

Benjamin Franklin

Accursed from birth they be
Who seek to find monogamy,
Pursuing it from bed to bed
I think they would be better dead.

Dorothy Parker

Now it is behoovely thing to tell which been the deadly sins. . . .Of the root of these seven sins then is Pride, the general root of all harms; for of this root springeth certain branches, as Ire, Envy, Accidie or Sloth, Avarice or Coveitise, Gluttony, and Lechery.

Chaucer

If you would not step into the harlot's house, do not go by the harlot's door.

Thomas Secker

From the moment a man thinks about committing a sin, he is faithless to God.

Midrash

All have sinned, and come short of the glory of God.

The Bible

Even a saint sins at least seven times a day.

Polish proverb

How many are there who do not sin from lack of desire or lack of occasion?

Joseph Roux

Sin is whatever obscures the soul.

André Gide

Old Time Religion

We shall never understand anything of our Lord's preaching and ministry unless we continually keep in mind what exactly and exclusively his errand was in this world. Sin was his errand in this world, and it was his only errand. He would never have been in this world, either preaching or doing anything else, but for sin. He could have done everything else for us without coming down into this world at all; everything else but take away our sin.

Alexander Whyte

Too many Christians envy the sinners their pleasure and the saints their joy, because they don't have either one.

Martin Luther

The Puritan Christian held, incredible as it may seem, that morals are more important than athletics, business or art; that the good life must be founded on virtue.

Ralph B. Perry

As society is now constituted, a literal adherence to the moral precepts scattered throughout the Gospels would mean sudden death.

Alfred North Whitehead

"Sin" is a seldom-used word today. But whether the word turns us on or off doesn't matter; it does not alter the truth, whatever we think. If my hangups and negatives are called "sin" by our Lord, then sin it is.

Robert Turnbull

Sins which are against the Creator, i.e. against Faith, Hope, Charity and the virtue of Religion, are the most grievous of all.

Christopher J. Wilmot

The historical Jesus has a different category of sins from that of the Old Testament or of Paul or of ecclesiastical writers after him. The sins which occupied the attention of Jesus were hypocrisy, worldliness, intolerance, and selfishness. The sins which occupy the principal attention of the Church. . .are impurity, murder, the drinking of alcohol, swearing, the neglect of the Church's services and ordinances.

Robert Keable

Men never do evil so completely and cheerfully as when they do it from a religious conviction.

Blaise Pascal

Man can emancipate himself from his Creator and make himself his own lord. That is what the Bible calls sin.

Emil Brunner

176

Christ didn't waste His time trying to change the social order. Christ spent all His time fighting sin. Therefore it behooves the witnesses of Christ to say that we do not have to abolish capitalism and establish socialism or communism, that sin can flourish under those systems as well. Christianity is not opposed to any social order, but to sin.

John H. McComb

One reason sin flourishes is that it is treated like a cream puff instead of a rattlesnake.

Billy Sunday

To call themselves "miserable sinners" is with any people a kind of religious good manners, just as a man inscribes himself "your humble servant."

J. A. Spender

There is none good but one, that is, God.

The Bible

Original Sin

For I fear I have nothing original in me—excepting original sin.

Thomas Campbell

Some psychological and sociological conditioning occurs in every man's life and this affects the decisions he makes. But we must resist the modern concept that all sin can be explained merely on the basis of conditioning.

Francis A. Schaeffer

Of Man's first disobedience, and the fruit
Of that forbidden tree whose mortal taste
Brought death into the world, and all our woe.

John Milton

Our sinful status is in our very creatureliness, not in our specific deeds.

C. S. Lewis

Sin is to be regarded as neither a necessity of man's nature nor yet as a pure caprice of his will.

Reinhold Niebuhr

God makes all things good; man meddles with them and they become evil.

Jean-Jacques Rousseau

Even as the holy and the righteous cannot rise beyond the highest which is in each one of you, so the wicked and the weak cannot fall lower than the lowest which is in you also.

Kahlil Gibran

I cannot account for the existence of evils by any rational method. To want to do so is to be co-equal with God. I am therefore humble enough to recognize evil as such. And I call God long-suffering and patient precisely because He permits evil in the world. I know that he has no evil.

Mohandas Gandhi

There is no explanation for evil. It must be looked upon as a necessary part of the order of the universe. To ignore it is childish; to bewail it senseless.

W. Somerset Maugham

All that is in the world, the lust of the flesh, and the lust of the eyes, and the pride of life, is not of the Father, but is of the world.

The Bible

When man by his own free will sinned, then sin being victorious over him, the freedom of his will was lost. . .he who is the servant of sin is free to sin. And hence he will not be free to do right until, being freed from sin.

Saint Augustine of Hippo

What is it inside us that lies, whores, steals and murders?

Georg Büchner

Sin a description of our entire situation, one of separation from God, alienation from him, arising out of our rebellion, our refusal to do his will, our insistence upon following our own wills.

Robert M. Brown

It is one thing to perceive this or that particular deed to be sinful. . .and another thing to feel sin within us independent of particular actions.

Samuel T. Coleridge

But however much you may advance in the love of God and of your neighbor, and in true piety, do not imagine as long as you are in this life, that you are without sin.

Saint Augustine of Hippo

As Christians, we do not have to renounce everything that gives pleasure to the senses. But we do have to moderate our use of sense pleasures. Original sin has left us easy marks for the allurements of sense.

John C. Ford

Let no man presume to think that he can devise any plan of extensive good, unalloyed and unadulterated with evil.

Charles C. Colton

We have altogether a confounded, corrupt, and poisoned nature, both in body and soul; throughout the whole man is nothing that is good.

Martin Luther

There is no belief in a supernatural source of evil is not necessary; men alone are quite capable of every wickedness.

Joseph Conrad

There are two infinities in this world: God up above, and down below, human baseness.

Edmond and Jules de Goncourt

It is easier to denature plutonium than to denature the evil spirit of man.

Albert Einstein

Depravity of will and corruption of nature are transmitted wherever life itself is transmitted.

Walter Rauschenbusch

We are utterly indisposed, disabled, and made opposite to all good, and wholly inclined to all evil.

Westminster Confession of Faith

Man of himself and his own is nothing, has nothing, can
do and is capable of nothing, but only infirmity, evil and
wickedness.

Theologia Germanica

Every one of us is a sinner. We are men, not gods.

Petronius Arbiter

I believe human nature doesn't change. I believe very strongly
in original sin.

John Lukacs

P

Passions
Peace
Penance
Pride
Punishment
Purity

Passions

On life's vast ocean diversely we sail,
Reason the card, but Passion is the gale.

Alexander Pope

Sin always comes openly and can at once be grasped by means
of the senses.

Franz Kafka

They that are after the flesh do mind the things of the flesh;
but they that are after the Spirit, the things of the Spirit. For
to be carnally minded is death.

The Bible

The most violent appetites in all creatures are lust and hunger:
the first is a perpetual call upon them to propagate their kind,
the latter to preserve themselves.

Joseph Addison

A man may commit adultery with a woman knowing well who
she is, but not of free choice, because he is under the influence of passion. In that case he is not an unjust man, though
he has done an injustice.

Aristotle

Whatever weakens your reason, impairs the tenderness of your conscience, obscures your sense of God, or takes away the relish of spiritual things; in short, whatever increases the strength and authority of your body over your mind—that thing is sin to you.

Susannah Wesley

Every person that does any evil, that gratifies any passion, is sufficiently punished by the evil he has committed, by the passions he serves, but chiefly by the fact that he withdraws himself from God, and God withdraws Himself from him.

John Sergieff of Cronstadt

Be grateful to your parents; had they not been tempted, you wouldn't be here.

The Talmud

Envy and fear are the only passions to which no pleasure is attached.

John C. Collins

It is with our passions, as it is with fire and water, they are good servants but bad masters.

Roger L'Estrange

When the passions become masters, they are vices.

Blaise Pascal

The soul that has been created for no other end than to love God, and to live in union with Him, will never be able to find peace or happiness in sensual enjoyments; God alone can make it perfectly content.

Saint Alphonsus de Liguori

We are n'er like angels till our passion dies.

Thomas Dekker

Peace

It is obvious from faith in Holy Scripture that no one can sin without weakening or disturbing peace with God and in consequence with every creature.

John Wycliffe

I couldn't live in peace if I put the shadow of a wilful sin between myself and God.

George Eliot

Sin is a tyrant. It exiles a man from himself and from his conscience and sends him elsewhere, anywhere, everywhere in his search for peace and rest.

Ignatius Smith

The wicked are like the troubled sea, when it cannot rest, whose waters cast up mire and dirt. There is no peace, saith my God, to the wicked.

The Bible

The worst bondage is exile from peace of mind.

The Talmud

Five great enemies to peace inhabit with us: viz., avarice, ambition, envy, anger and pride. If those enemies were to be banished, we should infallibly enjoy perpetual peace.

Petrarch

When he has no lust, no hatred, a man walks safely among the things of lust and hatred.

Bhagavadgita

Penance

The sin they do by two and two they must pay for one by one.
Rudyard Kipling

When the nobility sin, the poor folk atone.
German proverb

Man's sin problem is never cured until his alienation from
God is overcome, until the rebellion of the human against the
divine is ended, until God and man are brought back together.
                                        Myron S. Augsburger

They enslave their children's children who make compromise
with sin.
                                        James Russell Lowell

If the wicked will turn from all his sins that he hath committed, and keep all my statutes, and do that which is lawful and
right, he shall surely live, he shall not die.
                                        The Bible

God be merciful to me a sinner.
                                        The Bible

Pride

Of all evil traits, none vulgarizes a person more than pride, so
that he cannot rise toward the majesty of the spiritual. Whoever yearns for the light of God to illumine his soul must
despise pride so that he will literally feel its defilement.
                                        Abraham I. Kook

Chaste women are often proud and forward, as presuming upon the merit of their chastity.

Francis Bacon

Pride and conceit were the original sin for man.

Alain R. Lesage

Whoso walketh in haughty pride repels the presence of God.

The Talmud

Compassion is the root of religion; pride is the root of sin.

Tulsi Das

False love is the stuff of all sin, for it is egoism, and egoism is rooted in pride, and pride is the primal sin.

Gerald Vann

All sins have their origin in a sense of inferiority, otherwise called ambition.

Cesare Pavese

Pride is the reservoir of sin.

Ben Sirach

Man is at variance with his fellow man by the force of the same pride which brings him into conflict with God.

Reinhold Niebuhr

190

Pride is a deeply rooted ailment of the soul. The penalty is misery; the remedy lies in the sincere, life-long cultivation of humility, which means true self-evaluation and a proper perspective toward past, present and future.

Robert Gordis

Whoever thinks he has not sinned carries great pride within himself and that is worse than sin.

Bahya ben Joseph ibn Pakuda

God does not listen to the prayers of the proud.

Hebrew proverb

Punishment

There shall be no reward to the evil man; the candle of the wicked shall be put out.

The Bible

Three fatal Sisters wait upon each sin: First, Fear and Shame without, the Guilt within.

Robert Herrick

Sins of the heart, such as infidelity, heresy, envy, hate, etc., are to be punished by the sword of the spirit, which is the Word of God.

Sebastian Castellio

We used to say that we were punished for our sin, as though
God were a judge on a bench who passed on the case and
meted out penalty. The truth goes for our sins, but by them. It
is our sins themselves that rise to slay us.

Harry E. Fosdick

All illness comes from sin. This everyone must take whether
they like it or not; it comes from sin—whether it be of body, of
mind, or of soul.

Edgar Cayce

The sinner sins against himself; the wrongdoer wrongs himself, becoming the worse by his own action.

Marcus Aurelius

The only things that are improved by breaking are the hearts
of sinners.

Anonymous

When God punishes sinners, He does not inflict His evil on
them, but leaves them to their own evil.

Saint Augustine of Hippo

The wicked shall fall by his own wickedness.

The Bible

Whoso committeth adultery with a woman lacketh understanding: he that doeth it destroyeth his own soul.

> The Bible

Let the wicked fall into their own nets.

> The Bible

The wicked shall fall into mischief.

> The Bible

The belly of the wicked shall want.

> The Bible

Many sorrows shall be to the wicked.

> The Bible

Adultery brings on early old age.

> Hebrew proverb

Sin kills the sinner and will continue to kill him as long as he
sins.

> Mary Baker Eddy

A person guilty of rape should be castrated. That would stop
him pretty quick.

> Billy Graham

Whoso shall offend one of these little ones which believe in me, it were better for him that a millstone were hanged about his neck, and that he were drowned in the depth of the sea. Woe unto the world because of offenses! for it must needs be that offenses come; but woe to that man by whom the offense cometh! Wherefore if thy hand or thy foot offend thee, cut them off, and cast them from thee: it is better for thee to enter into life halt and maimed, rather than having two hands or two feet to be cast into everlasting fire. And if thine eye offend thee, pluck it out, and cast it from thee: it is better for thee to enter into life with one eye, rather than having two eyes to be cast into hell fire.

The Bible

The way of transgressors is hard.

The Bible

He that swims in sin will sink in sorrow.

Anonymous

A wicked life leads to a wicked death.

Molière

The wages of sin is death.

The Bible

Purity

Not in the sky, not in the midst of the sea, not if we enter into the clefts of the mountains, is there known a spot in the whole world where a man might be freed from an evil deed. By oneself the evil is done, by oneself one suffers; by oneself evil is left undone, by oneself one is purified. Purity and impurity belong to oneself, no one can purify another.

Buddha

Unto the pure all things are pure.

The Bible

The body is the soul's image; therefore keep it pure.

Pope Xystus I

Purity of soul cannot be lost without consent.

Saint Augustine of Hippo

Who can say, I have made my heart clean?

The Bible

Only if it is quite immaculate can the heart enjoy itself.

Johann W. von Goethe

Purity is for man, next to life, the greatest food, that purity
that is procured by the law of Mazda to him who cleanses his
own self with good thoughts, words, and deeds.

Zend-Avesta

Purity is the sum of all loveliness, as whiteness is the sum of all
colors.

Francis Thompson

I don't like those who are "pure as snow"—for snow is not
long white and pure, but soon turns muddy and soiled.

The Riziner Rabbi

The sun, though it passes through dirty places, yet remains as
pure as before.

Francis Bacon

My strength of ten,
Because my heart is pure.

Alfred Lord Tennyson

R

**Repentance
Reputation
Resisting Temptation
Rewards**

Repentance

The Lord is not slack concerning his promise, as some men count slackness; but is long-suffering to us-ward, not willing that any should perish, but that all should come to repentance.

The Bible

Knowledge of sin is the beginning of salvation.

Seneca

The really unforgivable sin is the denial of sin, because, by its nature, there is now nothing to be forgiven.

Fulton J. Sheen

The first step toward the soul's recovery is the knowledge of the sin committed.

Seneca

Let us remember for our consolation that we never perceive our sins till we begin to cure them.

François Fénelon

God loves me even while I sin. But it cannot be said too strongly that there is a wrath of God against me as sinning; God's will is set one way and mine is set against it. And therefore, though he longs to forgive, he cannot do so unless either my will is turned from its sinful direction into conformity with his, or else there is at work some power which is capable of effecting that change in me.

William Temple

Reform must come from within, not from without. You cannot legislate for virtue.

James Gibbons

A man who has reformed himself has contributed his full share towards the reformation of his neighbor.

Norman Douglas

Who sins and mends commends himself to God.

Cervantes

Joy shall be in heaven over one sinner that repenteth, more than over ninety and nine just persons, which need no repentance.

The Bible

Every sin brings about a particular type of trembling in the soul, which does not cease until repentance has been made. When man repents out of love, the cosmic light of the world of unity shines upon him and everything is joined in oneness; evil joins with the good and raises it to even a higher value.

Abraham I. Kook

The seeds of repentance are sown in youth by pleasure, but the harvest is reaped in age by pain.

Charles C. Colton

Remorse sleeps during prosperity but awakes to bitter consciousness during adversity.

Jean-Jacques Rousseau

We are never so virtuous as when we are ill. . . . It is then a man recollects that there are gods, and that he himself is mortal . . . and he resolves that if he has the luck to recover, his life shall be passed in harmless happiness.

Pliny

Sin repented can still leave a crushing weight upon the soul, even one sin.

Frank J. Sheed

Repentance, I suppose, is nothing else than the sight, for a moment, of sin as God sees it.

W. M. MacGregor

Lord, often have I thought with myself, I will sin but this one
sin more, and then I will repent of it, and of all the rest of my
sins together. So foolish was I and ignorant. As if I should be
more able to pay my debts when I owe more; or as if I should
say, I will wound my friend once again, and then I will
lovingly shake hands with him: but what if my friend will not
shake hands with me?

Thomas Fuller

The repentant say never a brave word. Their resolves should
be mumbled in silence.

Henry David Thoreau

God pardons those who do through frailty sin,
But never those that persevere therein.

Robert Herrick

Our repentance is not so much regret for the evil we have
done, as fear of its consequences.

La Rochefoucauld

The repentance of man is accepted by God as virtue.

Voltaire

To many people virtue consists mainly in repenting faults, not
in avoiding them.

C. C. Lichtenberg

Indeed, sometimes I do repent
    And pardon to obtain,
But yet, alas, incontinent,
    I fall to sin again.

John Carelesse

The saints are the sinners who keep on trying.

Robert Louis Stevenson

God preserves the wicked to give them time to repent.

Comtesse de Ségur

The sinning is the best part of repentance.

Arabic proverb

Reputation

So good a thing is virtue that even its enemies applaud and admire it.

Saint John Chrysostom

There is no den in the wide world to hide a rogue. Commit a crime and the earth is made of glass. Commit a crime, and it seems as if a coat of snow fell on the ground, such as reveals in the woods the track of every partridge, and fox, and squirrel.

Ralph Waldo Emerson

He that walketh uprightly walketh surely: but he that per-
verteth his ways shall be known.

The Bible

I wore vice like a garment; now it is stuck to my skin.

Alfred de Musset

Those who are once found to be bad are presumed to be so
forever.

Spanish proverb

He that sweareth till no man trust him,
He that lieth till no man believe him,
He that borroweth till no man will lend him,
Let him go where no man knoweth him.

Hugh Rhodes

The sin lieth in the scandal.

Asphra Behn

God will accept repentance for all sins except one: giving
another man a bad name.

Zohar

Resisting Temptation

Sin and dandelions are very much alike. To get rid of them is a lifetime fight, and you never quite win it.

William A. White

The ordeal of virtue is to resist all temptation to evil.

Thomas R. Malthus

It's much easier to resist temptation if you're broke.

Anonymous

Every moment of resistance to temptation is a victory.

Frederick W. Faber

There are several good protections against temptation, but the surest is cowardice.

Mark Twain (Samuel Clemens)

Assuredly, he, who is only kept from vice by the fear of punishment, is in no wise acted on by love, and by no means embraces virtue. For my own part, I avoid or endeavor to avoid vice, because it is at direct variance with my proper nature and would lead me astray from the knowledge and love of God.

Benedict Spinoza

If the Evil Impulse says: "Sin—God will forgive you," don't heed it.

The Talmud

Never put yourself in temptation's path; for even King David could not resist it.

The Talmud

Watch and pray, that ye enter not into temptation: the spirit indeed is willing, but the flesh is weak.

The Bible

He who is without a wife dwells without blessing, life, joy, help, good, and peace—and without defense against temptation.

The Talmud

A woman's resistance is no proof of her virtue; it is much more likely to be a proof of her experience. If we spoke sincerely, we should have to confess that our first impulse is to yield; we only resist on reflection.

Anne de Lenclos

His master's wife cast her eyes upon Joseph; and she said, Lie with me. But he refused.

The Bible

From all inordinate and sinful affections; and from all the
deceits of the world, the flesh, and the devil, Good Lord,
deliver us.

> Book of Common Prayer

My son, if sinners entice thee, consent thou not.

> The Bible

Patience conquers the Devil.

> German proverb

But he who never sins can little boast
Compared to Him who goes and sins no more!

> Nathaniel P. Willis

It is easy enough to be prudent,
  When nothing tempts you to stray;
When without or within no voice of sin
  Is luring your soul away;
But it's only a negative virtue
  Until it is tried by fire,
And the life that is worth the honor of earth,
  Is the one that resists desire.

> Ella Wheeler Wilcox

A man is not honest simply because he had no chance to steal.

> Hebrew proverb

What makes resisting temptation difficult, for many people,
is that they don't want to discourage it completely.

Franklin P. Jones

Most of us keep at least one eye on the temptation we pray
not to be led into.

Anonymous

I can resist everything except temptation.

Oscar Wilde

Rewards

Earth reserves no blessing
For the unblessed of Heaven!

Emily Brontë

A good conscience is a continual feast.

Francis Bacon

There is no evil that does not offer inducements.
Vices tempt you by the rewards which they offer.

Seneca

No matter how great his trial may be, every saved sinner can always find reason for thanksgiving.

Philip E. Howard, Jr.

If one fights for good behaviour, God makes one present of the good feelings.

Juliana H. Ewing

There is no man who in his heart would not reverence a woman that chose to die rather than to be dishonored.

Thomas De Quincey

Blessed is the man that endureth temptation: for when he is tried, he shall receive the crown of life.

The Bible

A good man doubles the length of his existence. To have lived so as to look back with pleasure on life is to have lived twice.

Martial

The man who is pure of heart will find new thoughts whenever he meditates.

Rabbi Nahman of Bratslav

S

Sacrifice
Salvation
Seduction
See No Evil, Hear No Evil, Speak No Evil
Shame
Sins of Commission
Sins of Omission
Slander
Standards

Sacrifice

The soldier who dies to save his brothers reaches the highest of all degrees of charity, and this is the virtue of a single act of charity: It cancels a whole lifetime of sin.

Désiré Joseph Mercier

The righteous sometimes pay for the sinners.

Cervantes

But the sin forgiven by Christ in Heaven
By man is cursed always.

Nathaniel P. Willis

You cannot throw words like heroism and sacrifice and nobility and honor away without abandoning the qualities they express.

Marya Mannes

Vice has more martyrs than virtue; and it often happens that men suffer more to be lost than to be saved.

Charles C. Colton

How exhausting it is to be evil!

Bertolt Brecht

Virtue does not always demand a heavy sacrifice—only the willingness to make it when necessary.

Frederick Dunn

Virtue is like precious odours, most fragrant when they are incensed or crushed.

Francis Bacon

Salvation

The Old Testament Hebrew word that we translate "atonement" means literally "to cover up." The animal sacrifices were intended to "cover" a man's sins. In the New Testament, however, the meaning of atoning sacrifice is conveyed by the word "expiate," which means "to put away." The blood that Jesus shed in our behalf on the cross at Calvary does not merely cover up our sin, it puts away our sin as though it had never been committed.

T. W. Wilson

If any man sin, we have an advocate with the Father, Jesus Christ the righteous: and he is the propitiation for our sins: and not for ours only, but also for the sins of the whole world.

The Bible

It is not enough to want to get rid of one's sins. We also need to believe in the One who saves us from our sins. Because we know that we are sinners, it does not follow that we are saved.

C. S. Lewis

Wash thine heart from wickedness, that thou mayest be saved.

The Bible

Many sinners would not have been saved if they had not committed some greater sin at last, than before, for the punishment of that sin, hath brought them to a greater remorse of all their other sins formerly neglected.

John Donne

Don't try to deal with sin, for you are sure to lose. Deal with Christ; let him deal with your sin and you are sure to win.

Arthur H. Elfstrand

Say not thou, I will recompense evil; but wait on the Lord, and he shall save thee.

The Bible

The simplest word of faith is the deepest word of theology: Christ died for our sins.

James Denney

I am one of those who believe that a man may sin and do wrong, and after that may do right. If all of us who have sinned were put to death . . . there would not be many of us left.

Andrew Johnson

There is no evil in the world without a remedy.

Jacopo Sannazaro

He that is dead is freed from sin.

The Bible

A saint is a dead sinner, revised and edited.

Ambrose Bierce

Though your sins be as scarlet, they shall be as white as snow; though they be red like crimson, they shall be as wool.

The Bible

Seduction

Evil people want good people to be evil and thus resemble them.

Plautus

I grew in vice through desire of praise; and when I lacked opportunity to equal others in vice, I invented things I had not done, lest I might be held cowardly for being innocent, or contemptible for being chaste. With the basest companions I walked the streets of Babylon (the city of this World as opposed to the city of God) and wallowed in its filth as if it had been a bed of spices and precious ointments. To make me cleave closer to that city's very center, the invisible Enemy trod me down and seduced me, for I was easy to seduce.

Saint Augustine of Hippo

Among my people are found wicked men: they lay wait, as he that setteth snares; they set a trap, they catch men.

The Bible

There is a way which seemeth right unto a man; but the end thereof are the ways of death.

The Bible

We must not so much as taste of the devil's broth, lest at last he brings us to eat of his beef.

Thomas Hall

Those who have evil designs on others threaten themselves.

Hesiod

Whoso diggeth a pit shall fall therein.

The Bible

She deceiving, I believing;
What need lovers wish for more.

Charles Dedley

Every sin is the result of a collaboration.

Stephen Crane

See No Evil, Hear No Evil, Speak No Evil

Every minute you are thinking of evil, you might have been thinking of good instead, refuse to pander to a morbid interest in your own misdeed. Pick yourself up, be sorry, shake yourself, and go on again.

Evelyn Underhill

Be not overcome of evil, but overcome evil with good.

The Bible

The most effective defense against temptation is this: Shut your eyes.

Ibn Gabirol

Few love to hear the sins they love to act.

Shakespeare

Have you heard of the terrible family They
And the dreadful venomous things They say?
Why, half of the gossip under the sun,
If you trace it back, you will find begun
In that wretched House of They.

Ella Wheeler Wilcox

The biggest liar in the world is They Say.

Douglas Malloch

Believe nothing against another but on good authority; and never report what may hurt another, unless it be a greater hurt to some other to conceal it.

William Penn

When we talk about evil persons, this may give rise to evil thoughts, and hence, God forbid, to bringing evil into the world. Therefore, let us talk only about the good ways of righteous men, and so bring good into the world.

Rabbi Zechariah Mendel

Never tell evil of a man if you do not know it for a certainty; and if you do know it for a certainty, then ask yourself: "Why should I tell it?"

Johann K. Lavater

To speak ill of others is a dishonest way of praising ourselves.

Will Durant

God hates these three; the person who says one thing with his mouth and thinks otherwise in his heart; the person who could give evidence in another's favor, but does not do so; and the person who, being alone, sees his neighbor sin, and gives unsupported testimony against him.

The Gemarah

An evil-speaker differs from an evil-doer only in the lack of opportunity.

Marcus Fabius Quintilan

Evil-speaking is wicked; it is a restless devil, never making peace, but always living in strife.

Shepherd of Hermas

Shame

Every one that doeth evil hateth the light.

The Bible

Shame leaves us by degrees.

Samuel Daniel

Shame has a longer life than poverty.

Dutch proverb

Shame and guilt are noble emotions essential in the mainte-
nance of civilized society, and vital for the development of
some of the most refined and elegant qualities of human
potential—generosity, service, self-sacrifice, unselfishness
and duty.

Willard Gaylen

Sin's effect on the soul is to be measured neither by the guilt
nor by the temporal punishment inexorably fixed, but by that
deep sense of loneliness it brings with it.

Bede Jarrett

When we sin, we are all ashamed at the presence of our
inferiors.

Saint John Chrysostom

I never wonder to see men wicked, but I often wonder to see
them not ashamed.

Jonathan Swift

Not to be ashamed of sin is to sin double.

German proverb

So long as there is shame there is hope for virtue.

German proverb

Surely then shalt thou be ashamed and confounded for all thy wickedness.

The Bible

To do injustice is more disgraceful than to suffer it.

Plato

Where there is no shame, there is no honor.

African proverb

Sins of Commission

All the seven deadly sins are self-destroying, morbid appetites, but in their early stages at least, lust and gluttony, avarice and sloth know some gratification, while anger and pride have power, even though that power eventually destroys itself. Envy is impotent, numbed with fear, never ceasing in its appetite, and it knows no gratification, but endless self torment. It has the ugliness of a trapped rat, which gnaws its own floor in an effort to escape.

Angus Wilson

Pride, covetousness, lust, anger, gluttony, envy and sloth, are the seven capital sins.

Catechism of Christian Doctrine

222

Now the works of the flesh are manifest, which are these, adultery, fornication, uncleanness, lasciviousness, idolatry, witchcraft, hatred, variance, emulations, wrath, strife, seditions, heresies, envyings, murders, drunkenness, revelings, and such like: of the which I tell you before, as I have also told you in time past, that they which do such things shall not inherit the kingdom of God.

The Bible

The higher and nobler the virtue to which it is opposed the more grievous is the sin. . . . The most terrible and grievous of all sins are the hatred of God, despair, unbelief, formal heresy, blasphemy, and the like.

Christopher J. Wilmot

Out of the heart proceed evil thoughts, murders, adulteries, fornications, thefts, false witness, blasphemies: these are the things which defile a man.

The Bible

Fornication, and all uncleanness, or coveteousness, let it not be once named among you, as becometh saints; neither filthiness, nor foolish talking, nor jesting, which are not convenient.

The Bible

These six things doth the Lord hate; yea, seven are an abomination unto him: a proud look, a lying tongue, and hands that shed innocent blood, a heart that deviseth wicked imaginations, feet that be swift in running to mischief, a false witness that speaketh lies, and he that soweth discord among brethren.

The Bible

If anyone thinks that Christians regard unchastity as the great vice, he is quite wrong. The sins of the flesh are bad, but they are the least bad of all sins. All the worst pleasures are purely spiritual: the pleasure of putting other people in the wrong, of bossing and patronizing and spoiling sport, and back-biting: the pleasures of power, of hatred.

C. S. Lewis

There are only three sins—causing pain, causing fear, causing anguish. The rest is window dressing.

Roger Caras

Lust . . . is both prevalent and reprehensible; but it may be doubted whether it does as much harm in the world day by day as the less socially disreputable misdemeanors of anger and envy.

Aelred Graham

All the wants which disturb human life, which make us un-
easy to ourselves, quarrelsome with others, and unthankful
to God, which weary us in vain labors and foolish anxieties,
which carry us from project to project, from place to place in
a poor pursuit of we don't know what, are the wants which
neither God, nor nature, nor reason hath subjected us to, but
are solely infused into us by pride, envy, ambition, and
covetousness.

William Law

The word SIN in the Bible means something more than the
external works done by our bodily action. It means all the
circumstances that act together and excite or incite us to what
is done; in particular, the impulses operating in the depths of
our hearts.

Martin Luther

Sins of Omission

We sin from two causes: either from not seeing what we ought
to do, or from not doing what we see ought to be done.

Saint Augustine of Hippo

There is often a sin of omission as well as of commission.

Marcus Aurelius

Modern man . . . has so long believed that right and wrong were only differences in point of view, that now when evil works itself out in practice he is paralyzed to do anything against it.

Fulton J. Sheen

The chief cause of our misery is less the violence of our passions than the feebleness of our virtues.

Joseph Boux

A state of temperance, sobriety and justice without devotion is a cold, lifeless, insipid condition of virtue, and is rather to be styled philosophy than religion.

Joseph Addison

The worst sin towards our fellow creatures is not to hate them, but to be indifferent to them; that's the essence of inhumanity.

George Bernard Shaw

You need not choose evil; but have only to fail to choose good, and you drift fast enough toward evil. You do not need to say, "I will be bad," you have only to say, "I will not choose God's choice," and the choice of evil is already settled.

W. J. Dawson

All that is necessary for the forces of evil to win in the world is for enough good men to do nothing.

Edmund Burke

A person may sometimes have a clear conscience simply because his head is empty.

Ralph W. Sockman

The cruelest lies are often told in silence.

Robert Louis Stevenson

He who does no good does evil enough.

Richard C. Trench

The omission of good is no less reprehensible than the commission of evil.

Plutarch

Slander

Slander is worse than weapons; for weapons hurt from near, slander from afar.

The Talmud

Calumny requires no proof. The throwing out of malicious imputations against any character leaves a stain which no after-refutation can wipe out. To create an unfavourable impression, it is not necessary that certain things should be true, but that they have been said.

William Hazlitt

This mixture of detraction and prophesy is the original sin of gossiping: and it has descended with rapid propagation to all races and languages among Christian men.

Henry E. Manning

Slander is in the same category with murder.

The Talmud

Whoever slanders a fellow man denies God.

Hebrew proverb

Into the space of one little hour sins enough may be conjured up by evil tongues to blast the fame of a whole life of virtue.

Washington Irving

There are different ways of assassinating a man—by pistol, sword, poison, or moral assassination. They are the same in their results except that the last is more cruel.

Napoleon Bonaparte

A lie can travel half way around the world while the truth is putting on its shoes.

Mark Twain (Samuel Clemens)

Calumny is like counterfeit money: many people who would not coin it circulate it without qualms.

Diane de Poitiers

Every one in a crowd has the power to throw dirt: nine out of ten have the inclination.

William Hazlitt

Some men are prone to steal, but all men seem prone to slander.

Hebrew proverb

Half the evil in the world is gossip started by good people.

Edgar Howe

The man who slanders hurts three people: the man slandered, the man to whom the slander is uttered—and himself.

The Talmud

He that flings dirt at another dirtieth himself most.

Thomas Fuller

The slanderer, like the liar and the hypocrite, will find no place in the world to come.

Hebrew proverb

Standards

Moral distinctions are (being) simply drowned in a maudlin emotion in which we have more feeling for the murderer than the murdered, for the adulterer than the betrayed: and in which we gradually begin to believe that the really guilty party, the one who somehow caused it all, is the victim, not the perpetrator of the crime.

Robert E. Fitch

Distinction between virtuous and vicious actions has been engraven by the Lord in the heart of every man.

John Calvin

No man of honour ever quite lives up to his code, any more than a moral man manages to avoid sin.

H. L. Mencken

If it be usual to be strongly impressed by things that are scarce, why are we so little impressed by virtue?

Jean de La Bruyère

It is not enough to serve God in the hope of future reward; a man must do right and avoid wrong because he is a man, and owes it to his manhood to seek perfection.

Maimonides

The free being who abandons conduct of himself, yields himself to Satan; in the moral world there is no ground without a master, and the waste lands belong to the Evil One.

Henri F. Amiel

The husband's sin remains on the threshold; the wife's enters the house.

Russian proverb

T

Tangled Webs
Temptation
Timing
Tolerance

Tangled Webs

Whatever is only almost true is quite false, and among the most dangerous of errors, because being so near truth, it is the more likely to lead astray.

Henry Ward Beecher

A liar begins making falsehood appear like truth, and ends with making truth itself appear like falsehood.

William Shenstone

At first, sin is like a spider's web; but in the end, it is like the cable of a ship.

Rabbi Akiba

Falsehoods not only disagree with truths, but usually quarrel among themselves.

Daniel Webster

Delusions, errors and lies are like huge, gaudy vessels, the rafters of which are rotten and worm-eaten, and those who embark in them are fated to be shipwrecked.

Buddha

Ye are of your father the devil, and the lusts of your father ye will do: he was a murderer from the beginning, and abode not in the truth, because there is no truth in him. When he speaketh a lie, he speaketh of his own: for he is a liar, and the father of it.

The Bible

We lie loudest when we lie to ourselves.

Eric Hoffer

I do myself a greater injury in lying when I do him of whom I tell a lie.

Montaigne

One lie gives birth to another.

Terence

A lie grows in size (as it is repeated).

Ovid

Falsehood has a perennial spring.

Edmund Burke

O, what a tangled web we weave,
When first we practice to deceive!

Walter Scott

There is no vice so mean, so pitiful, so contemptible; and he who permits himself to tell a lie once, finds it much easier to do it a second and third time, till at length it becomes habitual.

Thomas Jefferson

Temptation

It is good to be without vices, but it is not good to be without temptations.

Walter Bagehot

It is the law of our humanity that man must know good through evil. No great principle ever triumphed but through much evil. No man ever progressed to greatness and goodness but through great mistakes.

Frederick W. Robertson

The potter does not test cracked vessels, because to tap them even once is to break them; but he does test good vessels, because no matter how many times he taps them they do not break; so God tests not the wicked but the righteous.

Saying of the Fathers

The beginning of all temptations is inconstancy of heart and
little trust in God; for as a ship without governance is stirred
hitherward and thitherward with the waves so a man that is
remiss and that holdeth not steadfastly his purpose is diversely
tempted.

Thomas à Kempis

Those saints which God loves best,
The Devil tempts not the least.

Robert Herrick

Watch and pray, that ye enter not into temptation.

The Bible

Be sober, be vigilant; because your adversary the devil, as a
roaring lion, walketh about, seeking whom he may devour.

The Bible

One is always wrong to open a conversation with the devil,
for, however he goes about it, he always insists upon having
the last word.

André Gide

Most of the methods that Satan uses to confuse and tempt can
be very beautiful and very alert. He seems to be not the
enemy of God, but the uplifter and edifier of man.

Anonymous

It is good and profitable to good men to be tempted and troubled, as is shown by what the prophet saith: To him that is tempted and troubled, God saith, I am with him in tribulation; I shall deliver him, and shall glorify him. Let no man think himself to be holy because he is not tempted, for the holiest and highest in life have the most temptations. How much higher a hill is, so much is the wind there greater; so, how much higher the life is, so much stronger is the temptation of the enemy.

John Wycliffe

There hath no temptation taken you but such as is common to man: but God is faithful, who will not suffer you to be tempted above that ye are able; but will with the temptation also make a way to escape, that ye may be able to bear it.

The Bible

Temptation is woman's weapon and man's excuse.

H. L. Mencken

The woman who has never aroused a man's desire shouldn't boast of her chastity.

Montaigne

He who lives looking for pleasures only, his senses uncontrolled, immoderate in his enjoyments, idle and weak, Mara (the tempter) will certainly overcome him, as the wind blows down a weak tree.

Dhammapada

All men are tempted. There is no man that lives that can't be broken down, provided it is the right temptation, put in the right spot.

Henry Ward Beecher

Opportunity knocks only once, but temptation bangs on the door for years.

Anonymous

Blessed is he who has never been tempted; for he knows not the frailty of his rectitude.

Christopher Morley

Anybody can be good in the country. There are no temptations there.

Oscar Wilde

Virtue is insufficient temptation.

George Bernard Shaw

Timing

The chance to do evil is found a hundred times a day, and that of doing good once a year.

Voltaire

Descriptions of sin are what we want at the breakfast table, not admonitions against it.

Alexander Cockburn

It is easier to abandon evil traits today than tomorrow.

Hasidic proverb

Most virtuous women are like hidden treasures—safe only because they are not sought for.

La Rochefoucauld

The devil is a gentleman who never goes where he is not welcome.

John A. Lincoln

First secure an independent income, then practice virtue.

Greek proverb

It is much easier to repent of sins that we have committed than to repent of those we intend to commit.

Josh Billings

Fortunate indeed is that man who was able to maintain control of his carnal senses in the time of his youth.

Bhartrihari

When men grow virtuous only in old age, they are making a sacrifice to God of the devil's leavings.

Jonathan Swift

God bears with the wicked, but not forever.

Cervantes

Live mindful of how brief your life is.

Horace

Don't worry about avoiding temptation—as you grow older, it starts avoiding you.

The Old Farmer's Almanac

During the first half of life it is hard to avoid temptation, and during the second half it is even harder to find it.

Anonymous

Sin is a dangerous toy in the hands of the virtuous. It should be left to the congenitally sinful, who know when to play with it and when to leave it alone.

H. L. Mencken

Men's virtues have their seasons even as fruits have.

La Rochefoucauld

Unto each man comes a day when his favorite sins all forsake him. And he complacently thinks he has forsaken his sins.

John Hay

Cultivate vices when you are young, and when you are old they will not forsake you.

Anonymous

How foolish was my hope and vain
That age would conquer sin.

Charles Wesley

All are good at first, but few prove themselves to be so at the last.

Shu Ching

The passions of the young are vices in the old.

Joseph Joubert

Every saint has a past and every sinner has a future.

Oscar Wilde

Tolerance

One man's sin may be another man's duty and a third man's bliss. . . . A democratic community cannot recognize the category of sin, legislate against it and punish those for whom the proscribed action is not sinful.

Sidney Hook

Accepting one's life means also accepting the sin of others which causes us suffering, accepting their nerves, their reactions, their enthusiasms, and even the talents and qualities by means of which they outshine us.

Paul Tournier

They that endeavor to abolish vice, destroy also virtue; for contraries, though they destroy one another, are yet the life of one another.

Thomas Browne

Saints are intolerant of sinners, but none so intolerant as sinners just turned saints.

Anonymous

Everybody likes to see somebody else get caught for the vices practiced by themselves.

Marya Mannes

Were I to cut myself off from my brethren because of their sins, I would be alone.

Ibn Gabirol

He who separates himself from sinners walks in their guilt.

Martin Buber

If a man foolishly does me wrong, I will return to him the protection of my ungrudging love; the more evil comes from him the more good shall go from me; the fragrance of goodness always comes to me, and the harmful air of evil goes to him.

Buddha

There no doubt is good in all the bitter woes that come upon us, because evil cannot proceed from God.

Rabbi Israel Baal-Shem Tob

Hate the sin and love the sinner.

Mohandas Gandhi

Everyone in daily life carries such a heavy, mixed burden on his own conscience that he is reluctant to penalize those who have been caught.

Brooks Atkinson

V

**Vanity
Vengeance
Vice
Virtue**

Vanity

The purer the heart, the larger it is, and the more able it is to find room within it for a greater number of beloved ones; whilst the more sinful it is, the more contracted it becomes, and the smaller number of beloved it can find room for, because it is limited by self-love.

John Sergieff of Cronstadt

He who hates not in himself his self-love and that instinct which leads him to make himself a God, is indeed blind.

Blaise Pascal

Self-love is the great enemy which must be overcome. Self-love separates man from God, it blocks the channels of self-spending and self-offering, both toward God and toward man.

Anders Nygren

Killing an animal to make a coat is a sin.

Doris Day

A corroding and deadening sin is professionalism, which shows itself in an affected tone of voice, a studied manner, a use of conventional phrases, and an unholy familiarity with spiritual things.

John Watson

Virtue would not go to such lengths if vanity did not keep her company.

La Rochefoucauld

The conceited man is not a sinner but a fool.

The Chofetz Chaim

Some rise by sin, and some by virtue fall.

Shakespeare

The devil is an egotist.

Johann W. von Goethe

Vengeance

Soldiers! we have sinned against Almighty God. We have forgotten His signal mercies, and have cultivated a revengeful, haughty, and boastful spirit. We have not remembered that the defenders of a just cause should be pure in His eyes.

Robert E. Lee

Revenge is a fever in our own blood, to be cured only by letting the blood of mother; but the remedy too often produces a relapse, which is remorse—a malady far more dreadful than the first disease, because it is incurable.

Charles C. Colton

Wilful murder, sodomy, oppression of the poor, and defrauding laborers of their wages are the four sins that cry to Heaven for vengeance.

John McCaffrey

Anger and jealousy can no more bear to lose sight of their objects than love.

George Eliot (Mary Ann Evans)

Don't let us make imaginary evils, when you know we have so many real ones to encounter.

Oliver Goldsmith

There will be no more occasions when the world praises the manly husband who cleanses his honour in the vile blood of the adulterer.

Tirso de Molina

Vice

Vice goes a long way toward makin' life bearable.
A little vice now is relished by the best of men.

Finley P. Dunne

Most vices may be committed very genteelly, a man may debauch his friend's wife genteelly; he may cheat at cards genteelly.

Samuel Johnson

If vice were not such a great delight to the wicked, it would never exist!

Peire d'Alvernhe

Vice knows she's ugly, so puts on her mask.

Benjamin Franklin

What maintains one vice would bring up two children.

Benjamin Franklin

He conquered by weapons, but was conquered by his vices.

Seneca

One big vice in a man is apt to keep out a great many smaller ones.

Bret Harte

A silk thread begins as the weakest of things, the mucus of a worm; yet how strong it becomes when entwined many times! . . . So it is with transgressions: they grow strong with repetition.

Bahya ben Joseph ibn Pakuda

Vice only wounds people from time to time; but its visible characteristics affect them from morning to night.

> Denis Diderot

═══

Vice is a monster of so frightful mien,
As to be hated needs but to be seen;
Yet seen too oft, familiar with her face,
We, first endure, then pity, then embrace.

> Alexander Pope

═══

We are more apt to catch the vices of others than their virtues, as disease is far more contagious than health.

> Charles C. Colton

═══

Learning virtue means unlearning vice.

> Seneca

═══

Virtue and vice divide the world, but vice has got the greater share.

> Thomas Fuller

═══

Righteousness exalteth a nation: but sin is a reproach to any people.

> The Bible

═══

There is a capacity of virtue in us, and there is a capacity of vice to make your blood creep.

> Ralph Waldo Emerson

Who does not sufficiently hate vice,
Does not sufficiently love virtue.

                    Jean-Baptiste Rousseau

Virtue

The door to virtue is heavy and hard to push.

                        Chinese proverb

Virtue is the art of the whole life.

                        Philo

Prudence, justice, fortitude, and temperance, are the Four
Cardinal Virtues.

                    John McCaffrey

Virtue is not the absence of vices or the avoidance of moral
dangers; virtue is a vivid and separate thing, like pain or a
particular smell.

                    G. K. Chesterton

Sweeter than the perfume of sandalwood or of the lotusflower
is the perfume of virtue.

                    Dhammapada

Seldom indeed does human virtue rise;
From trunk to branch.

Dante

———

Wisdom and virtue are like the two wheels of a cart.

Japanese proverb

———

Virtue is praised, but hated. People run away from it, for it is ice-cold and in this world you must keep your feet warm.

Denis Diderot

———

Virtue commands respect, and respect is uncomfortable; virtue demands admiration, and admiration is boring.

Denis Diderot

———

What we should really beg of our neighbors is: "Forgive us our virtues."

Friederich W. Nietzsche

———

We know God will forgive us our sins; the question is, what will He think of our virtues?

Peter de Vries

———

Virtue carries a lean purse.

Japanese proverb

255

We do not stop being virtuous when we violate virtue, but when we stop believing in it.

Anonymous

I have seen men incapable of the sciences, but never any incapable of virtue.

Voltaire

A man can transform a fault into a virtue, if he only perseveres.

The Maggid of Dubno

Mortals that would follow me,
Love virtue, she alone is free;
She can teach ye how to climb
Higher than the sphery chime;
Or if virtue feeble were,
Heav'n itself would stoop to her.

Milton

No beauty leaves such an impression, strikes so deep, or links the souls of men closer than virtue.

Robert Burton

I believe long habits of virtue have a sensible effect on the countenance.

Benjamin Franklin

Who can find a virtuous woman? For her price is far above
rubies.

The Bible

Women's virtue is founded upon a modest countenance,
precise behavior, rectitude, and the want of temptation.

The Hitopadesa

White Lies
Wickedness
Wine, Women, and Song

White Lies

The most hateful evil in the world is the evil that dresses itself in such a way that men can not hate it. The men that make wickedness beautiful are the most utterly to be hated.

Henry Ward Beecher

Woman's virtue is man's greatest invention.

Cornelia Otis Skinner

The devil can cite Scripture for his purpose.

Shakespeare

We shut our eyes to the beginnings of evil because they are small, and in this weakness is contained the germ of our defeat.

Samuel T. Coleridge

No man ever became extremely wicked all at once.

Juvenal

Little sins make room for great, and one brings in all.

Thomas Edwards

When thou art obliged to speak, be sure to speak the truth, for equivocation is half way to lying, and lying is whole way to hell.

William Penn

No notice is taken of a little evil, but when it increases it strikes the eye.

Aristotle

A half truth is a whole lie.

Yiddish proverb

Wickedness

Wickedness, like a flood, is like to drown our English world. It begins already to be above the tops of the mountains; it has almost swallowed up all; our youth, middle age, old age, and all, are almost carried away of this flood.

John Bunyan

There is a method in man's wickedness—
It grows up by degree.

Beaumont

The wicked bend their bow,
they make ready their arrow upon the string,
that they may privily shoot at the upright in heart.
The Bible

He that has led a wicked life, is afraid of his own memory.
Thomas Fuller

Thou knowest all the wickedness which thine heart is privy
to.
The Bible

Thine own wickedness shall correct thee, and thy back-
slidings shall reprove thee.
The Bible

Seven pits lie open before the good man—and he escapes:
only one lies before the wicked man—and he falls into it.
The Talmud

An evil disposition never finds joy through wrongdoing.
Giambattista C. Giraldi

Wine, Women, and Song

The sons of the divvel,
In alcohol are swimmin'
But the straight and narrow path for me;
It's all very well
Bookin' certs and chasin' women,
But the straight and narrow path for me.

English Popular Song

When a man is enjoying the gratification of sexual passion or the pleasure of eating he ought to feel the presence of poison and be reminded of original sin. That is the nature of every enjoyment connected with lust.

Nicholas Berdyaev

For the mind that yields to the uncontrolled and wandering senses, carries away his wisdom just as a boat on water is carried away by wind.

Bhagavad Gita

God has bidden us to refrain not only from other men's wives, but also from the common women of the town; when two bodies are joined together, He says, they are made into one. So the man who plunges into filth must of necessity with filthiness be stained.

Lactantius

He who sins is still worse if he rejoices in his loss of righteousness.

Saint Augustine of Hippo

Pleasure's a sin, and sometimes sin's a pleasure.

George N. Gordon

Wine and women put wise men on guard.

Ben Sirach

The company of women improves men's manners but impairs their morals.

Montesquieu

If girls were not pretty, men would completely ignore temptation.

Hebrew proverb

The lips of a strange woman drop as a honeycomb, and her mouth is smoother than oil.

The Bible

In the intercourse of life, we please more often by our vices than by our virtues.

La Rochefoucauld

265

We must acknowledge that there is such a thing as "the pleasures of sin"—temptation would not be so strong if this were not true. The answer is to make our love of God stronger than all temptation, and in that way to lead the good Christian life.

Peter Marshall

Come, let us take our fill of love until the morning: let us solace ourselves with loves. For the goodman is not at home, he is gone a long journey.

The Bible

The heart and the eyes are like spies for the body: the eye sees, the heart covets, and the body commits the transgression.

Rashi

Even a shower of gold cannot secure satisfaction of our passions. He who realizes that passions give brief enjoyment and can produce much distress, is wise.

Dhammapada

Index